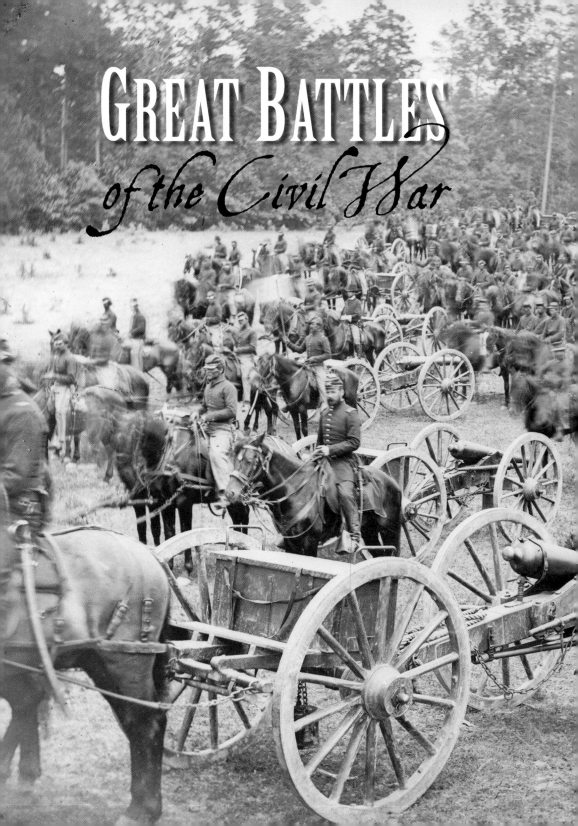

GREAT BATTLES
of the Civil War

GREAT BATTLES
of the Civil War

Swafford Johnson

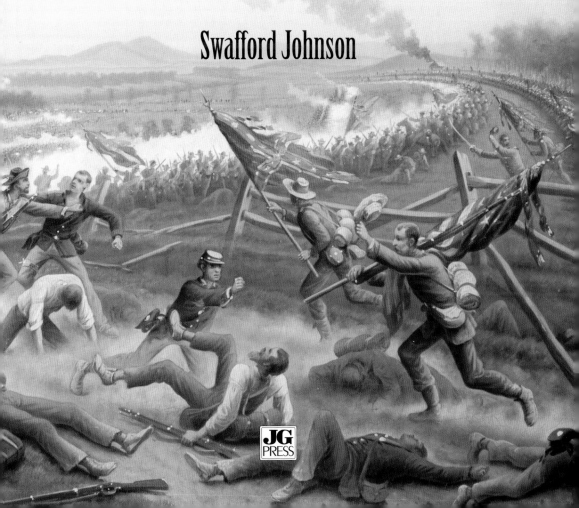

JG
PRESS

Published by World Publications Group, Inc.
140 Laurel Street
East Bridgewater, MA 02333
www.wrldpub.com

Jacket design by Kevin Ullrich

Printed in China by Toppan Leefung Printing Limited

Acknowledgements
The publisher would like to thank the following people who
helped in the preparation of this book: Don Longabucco
designer; Rita Longabucco, picture research; Cynthia Klein,
indexer; and John Kirk, editor.

Picture Credits
All photographs courtesy of the Library of Congress or the
National Archives.

Page 1: *Horatio G. Gibson's Batteries C and G, 3rd US
Artillery, Fair Oaks, VA.*

Pages 2-3: Gettysburg: The First Day, *James Walker, 1863.
Painted for Confederate officer, Fitzhugh Lee, Walker's artwork
depicts Confederate Army troops advancing on the town of
Gettysburg July 1, 1863. (West Point Museum Collection).*

Pages 4-5: *Union cavalrymen of Pleasonton's Corps in 1863.*

CONTENTS

SOUTHERN VICTORIES 7

   THE OPENING GUNS 8

   FIRST AND SECOND MANASSAS 14

   JACKSON'S VALLEY CAMPAIGN 30

   FREDERICKSBURG 42

   CHANCELLORSVILLE 54

   CHICKAMAUGA 66

   EPILOGUE: THE END OF THE CONFEDERACY 78

NORTHERN VICTORIES 83

   THE NORTH GOES TO WAR 84

   SHILOH 88

   VICKSBURG 98

   GETTYSBURG 112

   TOTAL WAR 134

   PETERSBURG 146

INDEX 158

Southern Victories

THE OPENING GUNS

On 20 December 1860, a convention of delegates meeting in Charleston, South Carolina, unanimously voted to pass this ordinance.

We, the people of the State of South Carolina, in Convention assembled, do declare and ordain, and it is hereby declared and ordained, that the ordinance adopted by us in Convention, on the 23rd day of May, in the year of our Lord 1788, whereby the Constitution of the United States of America was ratified, and also all Acts and parts of Acts of the General Assembly of this State ratifying the amendments of the said Constitution, are hereby repealed, and that the union now subsiding between South Carolina and other States under the name of the United States of America is hereby dissolved.

It happened at last, the thing long predicted and long feared: the United States, which had fought so fiercely for nationhood and felt themselves to be the hope of the world, were beginning to fall apart. A state had seceded from the Union. Others were ready to follow its lead.

The issues swirling around slavery had, beginning from the inception of the country, tended increasingly to split the nation along sectional lines. Among other corollary issues were the contending doctrines of federalism and of states' rights. Federalism, strongest in the North, proclaimed the primacy of the federal government and its laws; while states' rights doctrine, strongest in the South, upheld the primacy of each state's government and the states' right to nullify Federal laws they did not like – and, in extremity, to sever their bonds with the Union entirely.

Thus over the years two sections of the country pulled apart in economy (the North was more industrialized), in temperament and in culture. On both sides, fear and suspicion gradually supplanted goodwill and reason. Eventually the situation had grown out of control of even the wisest of men. The divisiveness came to a head with the election of Abraham Lincoln, whom the South perceived as a rabid abolitionist. In reality, Lincoln was comparatively a moderate on the issue. He regarded slavery as a great evil, writing at one point, "If slavery is not wrong, then nothing is wrong." But

Below: *An early cotton gin. It made cotton the staple crop of the South, increasing the demand for slaves.*

Opposite: *Jefferson Davis, US senator and former cabinet officer, became president of the CSA.*

Lincoln was willing to go to any lengths to resolve tensions peacefully; if that meant tolerating slavery for the time being, he would tolerate it.

By the time of Lincoln's inauguration, on 4 March 1861, he was faced with a rival government of seven Southern states calling themselves the Confederate States of America: South Carolina, Mississippi, Florida, Alabama, Georgia, Louisiana, and Texas. Following the lead of South Carolina, these states had responded to Lincoln's election by seceding from the Union, had drawn up a constitution, appointed a president, and claimed all Federal property within their borders.

Lincoln's opposite, Confederate President Jefferson Davis, was already occupying his office and planning how best to take over Union garrisons in the South. There were three of these in Florida, far from the centers of government; it was on the fourth garrison that the attention of the whole country came to rest – Fort Sumter, in Charleston Harbor.

The importance and the vulnerability of Fort Sumter had become clear even before Lincoln or Davis had taken office. After South Carolina seceded, state authorities sent a commission to President James Buchanan to arrange for transfer of Federal property to the Confederacy. Buchanan, who was not entirely unsympathetic to the South, met the commissioners unofficially and told them he would not change the status quo in Charleston Harbor. But soon after this the status quo did change ominously. Acting on his own, Major Robert Anderson, Federal commander in the harbor, loaded his men on boats and took them from the old Revolutionary Fort Moultrie, near the mainland, to the more defensible Fort Sumter, an unfinished pentagonal brick edifice three miles out in the harbor. The significance of Anderson's move was

Above: *Major Anderson left Fort Moultrie on Christmas night 1860. The troops moved to Fort Sumter.*

Opposite: *A Currier & Ives print of the attack on Fort Sumter in Charleston Harbor, 12 April 1861.*

not lost on Confederate authorities. In January President Buchanan sent a boat of provisions to the fort, which was low on both food and munitions; the boat was fired on from the South Carolina mainland and turned back. The state government decreed that no supplies of any kind were to be allowed in. By the time Lincoln took office Fort Sumter was isolated and running out of food.

The president decided neither to abandon the fort nor to initiate hostilities, but rather to send a boatload of provisions to the garrison. In notifying the governor of South Carolina of that action Lincoln was in effect challenging the Confederates to respond: if hostilities were to begin, it must be the South's doing. The next day, 7 April, the response came: General Pierre G T Beauregard, Confederate commander in Charleston, cut off communications between Charleston and the fort and began to organize Confederate forces in the harbor. On 11 April Beauregard sent a demand for evacuation to Major Anderson. Sumter's commander, realizing the terrible momentum that was gathering about his command, replied that he would evacuate on 15 April unless he was attacked or received further orders from Washington. Suspecting, correctly, that this would not satisfy the Confederate authorities, Anderson assured the aides who delivered the ultimatum, "Gentlemen, if you do not batter the fort to pieces about us, we shall be starved out in a few days."

The momentum of events rolled on, pulled by the seem-

ingly irresistible magnet of war. At 3:20 in the morning on 12
April the next note came to Major Anderson: We have the
honor to notify you that [Beauregard] will open the fire . . . in
one hour from this time." Greatly upset, Major Anderson
accompanied the Confederate messengers back to their
boat. Pressing their hands in farewell, he choked, "If we never
meet in this world again, God grant that we may meet in the
next." (Among Anderson's acquaintances on the other side
was Beauregard, his artillery instructor at West Point.)

Surrounding Fort Sumter in a wide circle on the mainland
and islands around the harbor, the guns of the Confederacy
were aimed and ready. Learning of Anderson's final words,
General Beauregard sent firing orders at about four in the
morning to Captain George S James and the James Island battery. Captain James positioned his men. When they were
ready he turned to his friend Roger A Pryor and said to him,
"You are the only man to whom I would give up the honor of
firing the first gun of the war." Shaken, Pryor declined. At 4:30
in the morning of 12 April 1861, Captain James pulled the firing
lanyard of a ten-inch mortar, and the first shot of the war
arched into the sky.

It was not until after daylight that Federal guns began re-
sponding from within the fort. The slow rate of return fire
showed the Confederates that the Federals were low on
ammunition and were mounting only token resistance. After
three hours of steady firing there were no casualties to either
side.

Three Federal warships appeared outside the harbor in
midmorning. The defenders in the fort cheered and flag
salutes were exchanged, but after a few hours the ships
turned and sailed away. Federal firing ceased at dusk. All
through the night the Confederate batteries kept up their
pounding while the defenders anxiously tried to sleep. About
dawn on 13 April the batteries of Fort Moultrie began pouring
hot shot into the fort, and the effects were soon seen: the

Above: *Interior of Fort
Sumter during the
bombardment. The shelling
produced no casualties but
the defenders' position was
plainly impossible.*

Below: *The Confederate
commander of Charleston, P
G T Beauregard, accepted
the surrender of Fort Sumter
on 13 April. The Union
evacuated the next day.*

Union barracks, supposedly fireproof, were in flames. The weak Federal return fire slowed still further, to one shot every five minutes, as soldiers in the fort were detailed to fight the flames and try to keep them from spreading to the magazine. Shortly after noon, the flagstaff of the fort was shot away and quickly repaired. But soon the Stars and Stripes were hauled down and replaced by a white flag.

A detachment was sent by boat to offer aid to the fort. They arrived to find that they had been preceded by ex-Senator Wigfall of Texas, who had apparently rowed out on his own to demand surrender. Wigfall had appeared in front of one of the fort's gun embrasures, to the considerable surprise of the Federal gunners. They had finally pulled Wigfall in before he was killed by his own side's fire. The ensuing negotiations were confused, what with two separate Confederate delegations and Major Anderson's uncertainties and anxieties – he and his men were begrimed with smoke and cinders and near exhaustion. But the outcome was inescapable. The garrison had taken some 4000 shells in 34 hours of nearly continuous bombardment and the Federals had few shells left to fire in reply. Finally Anderson capitulated, saying he would evacuate Fort Sumter on 14 April. Beauregard generously agreed that the Federals could salute their flag with cannons before leaving. By that point there still had been no casualties on either side.

As an ironic fate would have it, men were nonetheless destined to fall as a result of this battle. As the Federals fired their salute to the flag on 14 April, some sparks from the smouldering fire in the fort set off a paper-wrapped cannon cartridge as it was being loaded. The explosion killed Private Daniel Hough and wounded five other soldiers, one of whom soon died. These were the first casualties of the Civil War.

The fighting seemed rather dashing and decorous at Fort Sumter; to the Southerners it seemed the realization of all their fantasies of how easy it would be to send the Yankees running. All over the South there was revelry, dancing in the streets, young men joining up in thousands, showing off their grand new uniforms and guns to their families. They dreamed of glory and immortality and the romantic excitement of battle.

But elsewhere in the South one woman of Virginia, living in sight of Washington, wrote eloquently of her fears and heartbreak:

I heard distinctly the drums beating in Washington. As I looked at the Capitol in the distance, I could scarcely believe my senses. That Capitol of which I had always been so proud! Can it be possible that it is no longer *our* capitol? Must this Union, which I was taught to revere, be rent asunder?

Right: *The Confederate flag flew over Fort Sumter throughout the war, despite several major Federal assaults. Confederate troops finally abandoned the ruined fort on 17 February 1865 before the approach of Union General Sherman's army.*

FIRST AND SECOND MANASSAS

After the fall of Fort Sumter war fever swept across the country – or rather, the two countries. President Lincoln called for 75,000 three-month volunteers to suppress the Southern rebellion. Four more states seceded – Virginia, Arkansas, Tennessee, and North Carolina. The border states – Delaware, Maryland, Kentucky, and Missouri – stayed shakily loyal to the Union, even though the latter three were slave states. Both sides expected a short war, to be won in one or two decisive battles. Certainly no one foresaw the four years of agony that were to come.

There were essential differences in the strategy and aims of the two sections. The more formidable task was the Union's – in order to conquer the South the North had physically to invade, occupy, and hold its entire territory. This involved unprecedented commitments of men and supplies. On the other hand, the Confederacy's strategy seemed to call

Left: *Robert E Lee during his tenure as Superintendent of the US Military Academy (1852-55). Offered command of all the Federal forces on 18 April 1861, Lee declined, having decided that he could not raise his hand against his home state of Virginia.*

Opposite: *The young army officer Thomas J Jackson would earn his nickname "Stonewall" at First Manassas, where his brigade stoutly defended its position on Henry House Hill.*

for the defensive. As Northern armies advanced into the South their supply lines would steadily become longer and more tenuous as their numbers shrank due to attrition and the necessity of guarding lines of communication. The South thus had the advantage of fighting on and for its own territory, and also had, theoretically at least, the advantage of *interior lines* (because an invading army must stretch around and contain its enemy, that enemy, being more compact, can shift its forces much faster to any point on the perimeter along interior lines of communications).

At the beginning of the war the South probably had at least as good a chance of winning its war as the American colonies had of winning theirs. Moreover, Jefferson Davis confidently expected Great Britain and France to come to the rescue of the Confederacy; the threat of losing Southern cotton, Davis said, would bring them to the Confederate cause. In this, as in many other things, Davis miscalculated seriously. Great Britain at the beginning of the war had enough surplus cotton to last two years, and after that time found other sources.

(However, a good deal of Southern trading with Great

Britain – cotton out, arms and supplies in – did go on during the war. The North imposed a blockade of Southern ports from the outset, but it did not become effective until later in the war. In the South, blockade-running developed into a fine maritime art.)

Nearly all the commanding generals on both sides were West Pointers; as the war went on, a number of untrained leaders of genius arose, among them Nathan Bedford Forrest. But since military tradition was stronger in the South, the Confederacy got more than its share of the best military minds of the time; at the beginning of the war the North had no one to compare to Robert E Lee, Jackson, the two Johnstons, and Beauregard. This superiority of Confederate generalship in the early part of the war was clear to all concerned in the two great battles fought on a little stream called the Bull Run, near Manassas, Virginia.

Having resigned his commission in the US Army – and in the process declining an offer to command all Union forces – Robert Edward Lee was made a general in the Confederate army and given overall command of operations in his beloved home state of Virginia. In June and July of 1861 Americans began killing one another: Union forces were defeated near Fort Monroe, Virginia, and Federal general George B McClellan secured the western countries of Virginia for the Union (this area was soon to achieve statehood). Lee sent 11,000 men under General Joseph E Johnston to Harpers Ferry, near the entrance to Virginia's Shenandoah Valley, and 22,000 under General Pierre G T Beauregard to Manassas Junction, some 25 miles southwest of Washington. Lincoln,

despite objection that Union forces were too green, ordered General Irvin McDowell to drive Beauregard away from the important Manassas rail junction. Most of McDowell's 30,600 men were three-month volunteers and militia; only 800 were regular army. In support of McDowell, General Robert Patterson was ordered to keep Johnston in the Shenandoah in order to prevent his reinforcing Beauregard.

On 16 July, McDowell began advancing from Washington toward what everyone seemed to know would be the first great convulsion of the war. Many felt it would be the last. Confidently, the Union soldiers shouted, "On to Richmond!" Accompanying the Federal army were swarms of reporters, Congressmen, ladies with parasols and picnic baskets, and assorted sightseers – all off to see the war as if it were a fireworks show.

Marching on the Warrenton Turnpike, McDowell's Federal army reached Centreville, near Manassas, Virginia, on 18 July. At that point Beauregard's forces were vulnerable, though McDowell had no idea of that fact. Since the Union forces had become highly disorganized during the march, McDowell did not try a fullscale offensive (if he had, it might well have been successful). Meanwhile, Beauregard had received thorough intelligence concerning Union dispositions from a network of spies in Washington. He asked General Johnston to bring his forces over from the Shenandoah, where Patterson proved unable to contest their departure. On the 18th McDowell did try a reconnaissance in force against Beauregard's right. After a brisk skirmish at Blackburn's Ford on the Bull Run, the Federals were sent running

Right: *Confederate and Union movements toward Manassas Junction on 18 and 19 July.*
Right bottom: *Troop positions on 21 July 1861.*

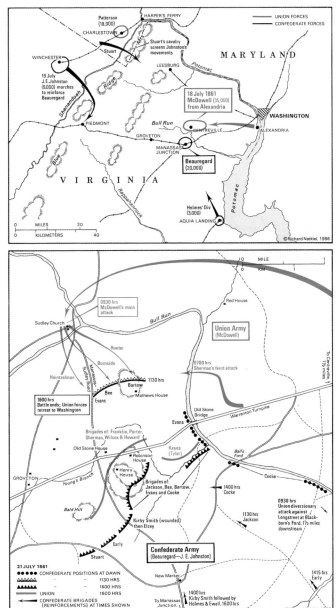

Opposite: *Confederate blockade-runners entering the harbor at St George, Bermuda. At first the Union blockade of the South was not very effective, but it became ever more so as the war progressed.*

back by the Confederates. The Southern commander in that skirmish was General James Longstreet, soon to be one of the great corps leaders of Robert E Lee's army. (In the South the affair at Blackburn's Ford is called the First Battle of Bull Run' to add to the confusion, the Northern names for the two large battles around the stream are the First and Second Bull Run).

McDowell's hesitation on the 28th allowed time for Johnston to move his 12,000 men east from the Shenandoah Valley. Most of that journey was made by railroad – the first

major strategic troop movement by railroad in history. Among Johnston's generals was a strange, laconic brigade commander named Thomas J Jackson.

McDowell and Beauregard had been classmates at West Point and had studied the same tactics. Perhaps for that reason, they made identical plans for an offensive on 19 July: feint with the left, attack with the right. If both had been successful, the results could have been strange indeed – after brushing past each other like a swinging door, the Con-

federates might have continued right into Washington and the Federals march into Richmond. But on the morning of the 19th, McDowell got his offensive underway first, and thereafter Beauregard and Johnston were on the defensive. McDowell made his feint on the Southern right, mounted a secondary attack on the enemy center, and took his right wing on a wide envelopment, marching the troops 15 miles through the broken and difficult landscape to attack the Rebel left flank.

Union general McDowell's plan was a perfectly good one, but it ran afoul of several problems. First, his troops were too inexperienced to execute with dispatch the intended wide envelopment of the Southern left flank. Second, Confederate observers on Signal Hill saw the movement and sent word to Beauregard: "Look out for your left; you are turned." Third, Beauregard had seen a cloud of dust on his left and realized the attack along the Warrenton Turnpike was a bluff to cover the move on his left. He began shifting divisions over to his left to oppose the oncoming Federals in the vicinity of Henry House Hill. As the Federals marched they could hear the whistles of the trains bringing Johnston's men to the battlefront. These arrivals were formed up on the railroad platform and marched directly into line.

Confident that every one of them could whip seven Yankees, the Confederate troops advanced from Henry House Hill towards the enemy. But then the Federals smashed into the Rebels, driving them back on to the hill. It seemed that the Federals were going to sweep the Rebels back down Henry House Hill. But defending that position was Thomas J Jackson and the brigade he had trained. He formed his men into a defensive nucleus on the hilltop. Seeing that stand, Confederate general Bernard E Bee entered history in his last moments of life. "Look at Jackson's Brigade," Bee shouted to his men, "It stands like a stone wall! Rally behind the Virginians!" And rally they did, stopping the advancing Federal troops in their tracks. And forever after, the general who led that stand would be called Stonewall Jackson, his men the Stonewall Brigade.

As Beauregard continued to strip his right and send men to the left, the Confederate line firmed up around Jackson on Henry House Hill. Finally Jackson led a counterattack on the Union right flank; sweeping around the hill in support rode the Rebel cavalrymen of young J E B ("Jeb") Stuart, another leader of that day destined for greatness. Jeb's men tore into a battalion of red-pantalooned New York Zouaves inflicting heavy casualties. At the most critical moment, just after two o'clock in the afternoon, on the Southern left, a Union artillery officer held his fire, mistaking blue-clad Rebel troops in his front for Federals; as a result, two powerful batteries fell into Southern hands and the Federals began to retreat. Now was Beauregard's great chance to pursue the enemy and annihilate them. However, at just that moment, Beauregard echoed the mistake of the Federal artillery commander: receiving a report that a large Federal force was moving on his supplies near Manassas, Beauregard pulled troops from his attack force to meet this threat. But the threat was a false alarm – it was Confederates marching towards the supplies, not Yankees. As Beauregard's advance slowed, dusk came on. The Confederacy had won the field that day of the first Manassas, but it was too late to pursue the enemy.

The Federals commenced an orderly retreat from the battlefield, moving up the Warrenton Turnpike. The Federal column, including numbers of civilian spectators who had not found the battle to be as much fun as they had expected, had to constrict to pass over a stone bridge over the Bull Run. Suddenly a Rebel battery dropped a few shells into the dense column near the bridge. There was an instant panic that quickly snowballed into a chaotic rout. By 22 July, Washington was inundated with the broken remains of its great army, which had become a mob of jaded, dirty, and demoralized men.

On the Confederate side there was a great and understandable jubilation over the triumph at Manassas. But the victory led to a dangerous overconfidence. Rebel soldiers had been confirmed in their illusion of invincibility.

Perhaps the South should have studied the casualty figures; they would have found the Union army had not been seriously damaged. Indeed, by the later standards of the war the First Manassas was not a particularly bloody contest – the South had 387 killed, 1582 wounded, 12 missing, for a total of 1981 casualties of the 32,232 engaged; the Union suffered 418 killed, 1011 wounded, 1216 missing, for a total of 2645 casualties of 28,452 engaged. The contrast in the numbers of missing is notable; but the fact remained that the Union army was only marginally more hurt than the Confederate – and the North had virtually endless supplies of manpower, whereas the South was severely limited in that regard. The day after the First Manassas, a young Federal general named George B McClellan took command in Washington and from the shattered Union forces of the First Manassas began rebuilding the army.

As will be described in the next chapter, Stonewall Jackson went on to his Shenandoah Valley Campaign of summer 1862. During that operation, Jackson kept three Federal armies tied up in the Valley and thereby helped to stymie Union General McClellan's Peninsular Campaign on Richmond with his new Army of the Potomac. During the Seven Days Battles that surged around Richmond during McClellan's campaign, Confederate General J E Johnston, one of the heroes of the First Manassas, was severely wounded. Johnston was replaced by General Robert E Lee; it was Lee who finished the job of driving the Army of the Potomac away from Richmond and, before long, out of Virginia entirely.

After tying up the enemy armies in the Shenandoah and keeping them from reinforcing McClellan, Stonewall Jackson hurried east to join Lee in the Seven Days Battles. As soon as Jackson's forces left the Shenandoah, new orders went out from Washington: the three Federal armies that had futilely chased Jackson were to be consolidated into one army under General John Pope, who was then to march South from

Above: *Stonewall Jackson directs his brigade at First Manassas, where he earned his nickname.*

Below: *Union marines, stationed to defend Washington, march outside their barracks.*

Washington and draw the Confederate army away from Richmond. But the plan was soon changed in light of Union
failures in the Seven Days, and a new plan developed: McClellan was to move his forces around by water to unite with

Pope; with the resulting army of 130,000 men, the Federals
would descend into Virginia to annihilate Lee's army of
50,000. Federal intelligence estimates had more than
doubled Lee's actual numbers; in contrast, Lee had a per-

Opposite top: *Confederate artillery repels a Union attack at First Manassas.*

Opposite bottom: *Rebel Black Horse Cavalry under assault by Union Zouaves.*

Above: *Artist Alfred R Waud sketched Union General McClellan crossing Bull Run on 29 March 1862.*

Right: *General George B McClellan would regain command of the Union army after Second Manassas.*

fectly clear idea of the daunting prospect he was up against. It was the first great challenge of his career.

The new commander of the Confederate Army of Northern Virginia was an unusual man for a soldier. So soft-spoken, courtly, and religious was Lee that many of his soldiers dubbed him "Granny." It was not long before they saw him more accurately: this mild-mannered Virginian aristocrat was one of the most aggressive and brilliant fighting generals who ever lived. But it is a strange position he occupies. Later called by Winston Churchill "the greatest of Americans," Lee was a primary leader of a rebellion that aimed to destroy the United States. Yet he believed neither in slavery nor in secession, and was certainly patriotic enough before the war. Like many Americans of that era, Lee placed loyalty to this home state above loyalty to the United States. In his resignation from the US Army, Lee said he could not raise his hand against Virginians; if they seceded, so must he.

It was not long before Lee was virtually deified by his Army of Northern Virginia. Moreover, the Army of Northern Virginia had an outstanding staff of subordinates. The great Stonewall Jackson was known as Lee's right arm. In addition there were the over-cautious but hard-fighting James Longstreet, impetuous A P Hill, choleric Daniel H Hill, and 25-year-old Jeb Stuart, one of the greatest cavalry-men of all time, who ful-

Left: *General Robert E
Lee in his preferred
uniform – that of a
cavalry colonel. As
commander of the
Confederate Army of
Northern Virginia, he was
almost deified by his men.*

Opposite above: *At
Cedar Mountain, in the
first battle of the Second
Manassas campaign, A P
Hill halted a Union
advance under Nathaniel
Banks on 9 August.*

filled his function of being the eyes of Lee's army with extraordinary effectiveness and dash.

Such generals combined with a fighting body of the highest
spirit made for one of the great armies of history, one already
legendary during its own brief existence. But it is also true
that there were deep and abiding weaknesses in both the
command structure and army. Chief among these weaknesses was that both Lee and the Confederate government
paid too little attention to logistics, especially the need to
feed and clothe the army properly. For much of the war
Southern soldiers marched and fought hungry, ragged, and
often shoeless, even when the Confederacy had abundant
supplies. The availability of arms and powder was remarkably dependable throughout the war, but soldiers need more
than weapons to fight. Beyond that, Lee often gave vague
orders, leaving much leeway for his generals; with a subordinate of genius like Stonewall Jackson, the results could
be spectacular, but with lesser generals there were often mis-
understandings. And Lee arguably gave too much of his

attention to his beloved home state of Virginia, leaving large-
scale strategy to the unreliable attentions of Jefferson Davis
(though this was more the fault of Davis than of Lee).

But all these things were unknown in July of 1862. By then
Lee had driven McClellan from the gates of Richmond, but he
faced the prospect of a grand combination of McClellan and
Pope's forces that would, if successfully accomplished, spell
almost certain doom for the Confederacy. On 14 July Pope
began moving his forces south in Virginia, intending to take
over the railroad junction at Gordonsville and then attack
Lee, who for the moment was still protecting the Confederate
capital from further efforts by McClellan. An observer
watched Lee as he grappled with this daunting situation:

When contemplating any great undertaking or a vast strategic combination, General Lee had an abstracted manner
that was altogether unlike his usual one. He would seek
some level sward and pace mechanically up and down
with the regularity of a sentinel on his beat; his head would

be bent as if in deep meditation, while his left hand unconsciously stroked his thick iron-grey beard.

Soon Stonewall Jackson was summoned; Lee now knew what he was going to do. Jackson and A P Hill were ordered north with 24,000 men to confront Pope and draw him away from the safety of Washington. Above all Pope had to be dealt with before McClellan could reinforce him, and time was running short it that was to be done. As always, Lee had examined his opponent carefully and knew his man. In this case, he knew he was dealing not with a worthy opponent but with a blustering fool. This may be seen in Pope's first address to his new command, in which he crowed, "Let us understand each other. I come to you from the West, where we have always seen the backs of our enemies." Lee took an uncharacteristically angry attitude towards this particular opponent; the "miscreant" Pope, Lee said, must be "suppressed."

Jackson set off with his and Hill's divisions to execute Lee's orders. He first planned to smash Pope's vanguard at Culpeper, Virginia, then to defeat the rest in detail, one corps at a time. But due to unwonted slowness, Jackson fumbled this initial strategy. On 9 August the advancing Confederates found themselves opposed by General Nathaniel Banks at Cedar Mountain. The Federals came on strongly and pushed Jackson's men back, but a crashing counterattack by A P Hill ended the enemy advance.

Pope's advance had been slowed, but no more. And now McClellan began pulling his Army of the Potomac away from Richmond by water and moving to combine with Pope. The immediate threat to the capitol over, Lee moved with Longstreet's division to join Jackson and march to the east of Pope's army, trying to maneuver to a position between him and both Washington and McClellan. This plan miscarried; because of poor staff work and a surprise attack on Jeb

Below: General John Pope commanded Union forces at Second Manassas. General Lee considered him an unworthy opponent.

Overleaf: Federal troops, protected by a determined rear guard, begin their retreat at First Manassas.

Right: *A column of Federal cavalry along the Rappahannock River in Virginia in August 1862.*

Below: *A Union brigade fails in its attempt to force strongly entrenched Confederate troops from the woods at the battle of Cedar Mountain.*

Stuart's camp (18 August) that captured Lee's plans, the Confederates were unable to march east of Pope. Finally both armies came to rest facing one another across the Rappahannock River, both making probing attacks with their cavalry. The report came to Lee that McClellan was now five days away from the juncture with Pope. In effect, the Confederates were racing with McClellan to get to Pope first. At that critical juncture in the history of the Confederacy, the combination of Lee and Jackson first revealed the genius for which history remembers them.

For the first, but not the last, time, Lee contradicted an ancient and virtually ironbound rule of military strategy: do not divide forces in the face of the enemy. In this case, it was an enemy that outnumbered Lee 75,000 to 55,000. The extraordinary bold plan was this: holding Pope in place on the Rappahannock with Longstreet's thinly spaced forces, Lee sent Jackson and Jeb Stuart on a wide envelopment, first northwest, then east, around Pope's army. Jackson's command left on 25 August; his foot soldiers duplicated the feats of marching they had demonstrated in the Valley Campaign, when they earned the title "foot cavalry." On the first day they marched 26 miles, the second day 36 miles.

At least McClellan had the sense to expect the unexpected from Stonewall Jackson. In the ensuing days that led up to the convulsion of the battle of Second Manassas, General Pope resolutely refused to believe that Jackson was behaving in anything but a timid and predictable fashion.

Pope's first surprise came on the evening of 27 August, when Jackson's men swamped the Union supply dump at Manassas. There the hungry Confederates had themselves the feast of a lifetime. After torching the remaining supplies, Jackson and Stuart pulled their forces away and, as far as Federal intelligence was concerned, vanished into thin air. General Pope, finding Jackson unexpectedly on his rear and the Federal supply line at Manassas destroyed, pulled his army away to the north on 26 August. This was what Lee had been waiting for; he took Longstreet's corps away from the Rappahannock, marching to meet Jackson. Meanwhile, Pope's blustering confusions continued; insisting that Jackson was retreating toward the Shenandoah Valley, Pope vowed to find and destroy him. Finally the Union army of 75,000 men was concentrated squarely between Jackson's force of 24,000 and Longstreet's still-distant 30,000. Here was a golden opportunity for the North: crush Jackson and then

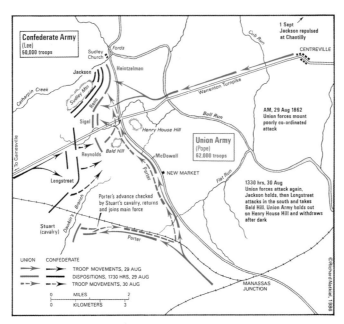

Left: *Map of Confederate and Union positions and movements at the Second Manassas.*

Opposite: *An A R Waud sketch of the defeat of the Federal Army of the Potomac under General Pope at the Second Manassas on 30 August 1862.*

turn on Longstreet. The trouble was, Pope could not find Jackson, despite frantic efforts to do so. Too, from start to very near finish, Pope ignored Longstreet entirely.

Nonetheless, with a large enemy between their divided forces the Confederates were in a desperate situation, one that might well have proven fatal if their opponent had possessed a modicum of sense. Jackson's problem was: how to hold Pope at bay until Longstreet arrived, how to attack, if possible, and still leave room to retreat. About 27 August Jackson found the place to do both those things – an unfinished railroad cut at the foot of Stony Ridge. It was an ideal defensive position, attackers having to make their way across a deep excavation. Behind the cut were mountain passes serviceable for retreat. On 27-28 August Jackson moved his forces to that position circuitously, in three detachments, and then literally hid his army in the woods behind the railroad cut.

On 28 August the Federals were in Groveton, unaware of Jackson's presence nearby. At that point Jackson made a historic gamble, a bigger one than Lee had made in dividing his army. With less than a third of the forces of the enemy, Jackson moved out and attacked the Federals, thereby revealing his position. It was a decision so bold as to seem foolhardy. The reason for it was that Jackson wanted to make sure Pope stayed away from strong defenses at nearby Centreville; if they pulled back to that position, the Federals could wait for the oncoming McClellan with impunity.

So Jackson moved out and struck the Federals near Groveton. A fierce skirmish developed as Pope turned his army to smash the supposedly retreating Jackson, meanwhile sending telegrams to Washington proclaiming victory over Jackson and saying Lee was in precipitate retreat to Richmond. Some of his officers tried to warn him of Longstreet's approach; Pope refused to listen. Now the Confederates were ready to engage the enemy before McClellan could arrive. The stage was set for the Battle of Second Manassas.

On the morning of 29 August 1862, General Pope threw 62,000 men against 20,000 Confederates, most of whom were again entrenched behind the railroad cut. All morning long the Union attacks continued; all were driven back with heavy losses. But the Confederates were increasingly desperate as the morning wore on.

As ammunition ran out, the Confederate defenders began hurling rocks at the attackers. General Maxcy Gregg walked up and down behind his troops, a sword of Revolutionary vintage in his hand, shouting "Let us die here, my men, let us die here!" Then, at about 11 in the morning, Longstreet's corp arrived on the Confederate right. In fact, Longstreet was squarely athwart a large gap in the Federal line; he could have fallen on the Union flank with devastating effect. But as was to be the case so often in the future, Longstreet was overcautious, worried about the Union corps on this right. Rather than mounting a fullscale attack, then, Longstreet moved some men over to make a demonstration on the Federal center. This sufficed to relieve the pressure on Jackson and to ensure the failure of Pope's offensive.

At the end of the day on 29 August Jackson pulled back from some of his advanced positions. Obtuse as ever, Pope declared that Jackson was retreating (the Federal commander was still oblivious to the presence of Longstreet). Pope ordered his men to pursue the enemy the next day. Lee encouraged Pope's illusions by letting some carefully-misinformed Federal prisoners escape back to their own lines; these returned prisoners assured Pope that the enemy was indeed retreating.

Next day, 30 August, the Federals, renewed their assault on the Southern lines, which now contained the entire Army of Northern Virginia. Lee let Pope hit Jackson's left, then sent Longstreet against the opposite Union flank. Longstreet remembered that morning:

A heavy fire of shot and shell was being poured into the thick column of the enemy, and in ten minutes their stubborn masses began to waver and give back. For a moment there was chaos; then order returned and they re-formed, apparently to renew the attack. Meanwhile my other eight pieces reported to me, and from the crest of the little hill the fire of twelve guns cut them down. As the cannon thundered the ranks broke, only to be formed again with dogged determination. A third time the batteries tore the Federals to pieces, and as they fell back under this terrible fire, I sprung everything to the charge. My troops leaped forward with exultant yells, and all along the line we pushed forward.

Now the Federal army was pincered between Longstreet and Jackson. Lee proceeded to swing his forces shut around the enemy like a gate.

Pope and his army were routed, but a stout Federal defense at Henry House Hill saved the army and made an orderly retreat possible. Lee and Jackson had created the first great victory of their immortal partnership.

There was much more to their success than a battle won, however. The Seven Days Battles, Jackson's Shenandoah Valley Campaign and the Second Manassas had really been one gigantic and ultimately victorious campaign of three months' duration. In that time Lee had sent two enormous Federal armies running back to Washington and virtually cleared Virginia of enemy forces. When Lee took command the North had been at the gates of Richmond. Now Lee was only 25 miles from Washington.

Yet in the end, the Second Manassas proved to be an incomplete victory. After driving the North from the field Lee tried to maintain the offensive, sending the corps of Jackson and Longstreet around the Federal west flank at Centreville. In this effort the exhausted Rebels discovered their enemy was still ready to fight. Jackson struck the Federals, but they resisted strongly even after two corps commanders were killed. In the end the Federals got away to Washington. On the next day Pope's forces were merged into McClellan's command, and that general once again took over operations in the East. Pope was never to command in the field again.

The Second Manassas was the first really devastating engagement of the Civil War. Now the soldiers and civilians of the contending nations were to learn the real costs of war. Confederate casualties were 1481 killed, 7627 wounded, 89 missing, a total of 9197 out of 48,527 engaged – 19 percent casualties. Federal losses were 1724 killed, 8372 wounded, 5958 missing, a total of 16,054 of the 75,696 engaged – 21 percent casualties.

Now Lee had to do something. He could not stay put; his army was in an exposed position near the enemy capital, where there were enormous masses of soldiers who would sooner or later be coming at him again. Lee knew he did not have sufficient strength to mount a siege of Washington. But it was not in his nature to pull back to safety near Richmond. Lee was above all an aggressive general; thus he decided to keep going, to invade Maryland. In this decision he underestimated his enemy and overestimated his own men. It was Pope, not the Federal soldiers, who had lost the Second Manassas; in battle the Northern men had fought with the same valor as their enemy.

JACKSON'S VALLEY CAMPAIGN

Stonewall Jackson showed his mettle in the Battle of Second Manassas. It was one of his greatest moments, but it was an earlier campaign in the Shenandoah Valley of Virginia that has forever stamped Jackson's genius in the annals of military history.

Thomas Jonathan Jackson had not seemed so promising at the outset of his military career. He arrived at West Point an awkward, taciturn mountain boy clad in rough homespun. With great effort he managed to rise from the bottom to nearly the top of his class during his four years. When the

Right: *Union General John Charles Frémont, commander of the Frederal Mountain Division in western Virginia, was defeated by Jackson in the Shenandoah Valley Campaign.*

Opposite: *General Thomas Jonathan ("Stonewall") Jackson, one of the greatest generals of the Civil War. His death on 10 May 1863 was a devastating blow to the Confederate cause.*

Civil War began he was a professor of mathematics and natural philosophy at the Virginia Military Institute and was already viewed as a strange character. He was a fanatical, brooding, and humorless Presbyterian, who never smoked or drank or played cards. He was obsessed with his health and with eccentric remedies: during the war he sucked lemons constantly, shunned pepper, claiming it made his left leg weak, and kept his right arm raised a good deal of the time, saying it improved the circulation.

So peculiar was Jackson that some of his own subordinates questioned his sanity. His obsessive secrecy drove his men close to madness themselves; not only did the enemy never know where Jackson was going, neither did any of his command, much of the time. But it was not long before everyone on both sides understood the military genius of Stonewall Jackson, and thereafter his men were happy to accept any

odd notion he devised. He was to become the indispensible right arm of Robert E. Lee, who described Jackson thus:

A man he is of contrasts so complete that he appears one day a Presbyterian deacon who delights in theological discussion and, the next, a reincarnated Joshua. He lives by the New Testament and fights by the Old.

The Shenandoah Valley of Virginia was one of the vitally important stretches of land in the Confederacy. It is the most fertile farmland imaginable, and was thus the breadbasket of the South. Beyond that, it was the ideal route for Confederate armies marching North for Maryland or Pennsylvania. To the Union, the Shenandoah was strategically useless; marching south in it took them nowhwere in particular. The Valley was important to the north only because it was so important to

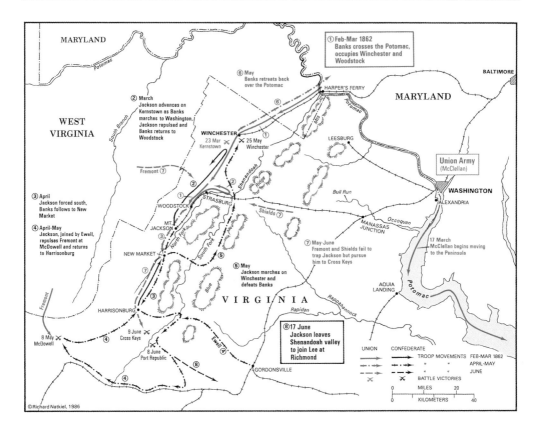

① Feb-Mar 1862
Banks crosses the Potomac,
occupies Winchester and
Woodstock

② March
Jackson advances on
Kernstown as Banks
marches to Washington,
Jackson repulsed and
Banks returns to
Woodstock

③ April
Jackson forced south,
Banks follows to New
Market

④ April-May
Jackson, joined by Ewell,
repulses Fremont at
McDowell and returns
to Harrisonburg

⑤ May
Jackson marches on
Winchester and
defeats Banks

⑥ May
Banks retreats back
over the Potomac

⑦ May-June
Fremont and Shields fail to
trap Jackson but pursue
him to Cross Keys

⑧ 17 June
Jackson leaves
Shenandoah valley
to join Lee at
Richmond

17 March
McClellan begins moving
to the Peninsula

Union Army
(McClellan)

UNION   CONFEDERATE

TROOP MOVEMENTS FEB-MAR 1862
            "   "   APRIL-MAY
            "   "   JUNE
✗   ✗   BATTLE VICTORIES

MILES   20
KILOMETERS   40

©Richard Natkiel, 1986

the Confederacy. Thus in October 1861 a Federal army occupied Romney, in the northern part of the Valley, and threatened Winchester; the Union was preparing to clear the Shenandoah of Confederates. In response, Stonewall Jackson and his brigade were sent to take charge of operations in the Shenandoah. With his Stonewall Brigade, some militia, and other troops, Jackson (now a major-general) commanded around 10,000 men. The main Union forces in the area were some 10,000 men under General Nathaniel P Banks.

After a winter of mostly fruitless maneuvering by both sides, Bank occupied Winchester in March of 1862, chasing Jackson's forces away and sending a Federal division south to occupy Strasburg. From that position Banks prepared to leave the Valley and join General McClellan's Federal Army of the Potomac, which was marching towards Richmond.

On 21 March Jackson learned of the planned Federal move from his cavalry commander, Turner Ashby. It was clear to Jackson as it was to his superiors that this must not happen: if Banks or any other major Union forces joined McClellan (a Federal army under McDowell was just east of the Valley and also slated to reinforce McClellan) they would gain overwhelming strength, and the Confederacy would be doomed. Lee, who at that time was overseeing operations in Virginia rather than commanding in the field, ordered Jackson to make a strategic diversion to keep Union forces, especially Banks's and McDowell's, in the Shenandoah and away from McClellan. In the process, he was to try to lead the Union high command into scattering their armies and also defend Rich-

mond from the west. In all those requirements Jackson was to prove successful beyond anyone's expectations.

Hurrying to keep the Federals in place, Jackson ordered Ashby's cavalry to attack Shields's division of Banks's army at Kernstown on 22 March 1862.

Next day Jackson arrived and followed up with his infantry (after searching his soul about fighting on Sunday). The Confederate attack went well for a while, until Shields moved some concealed forces into line. Then, outnumbered and low on ammunition, Jackson's men retreated, with Ashby covering the rear. Casualties in the fighting were disproportionate: the South had lost 700 of 4200 engaged; the Union 590 of 9000 engaged. It seemed a most unpromising beginning for Jackson's campaign.

In fact, Kernstown proved to be as good as a major victory for the South. Federal authorities assumed that Jackson's command was far larger than it actually was, and simply threw over the entire plan to reinforce McClellan, to that general's great disgust (for all his mistakes, McClellan understood better than his superiors in Washington that Jackson's campaign was a diversion). Orders went out from Washington: Banks and McDowell were to stay in the Shenandoah to deal with Jackson; indeed, some additional troops were stripped from McClellan for the purpose. At length there were three uncoordinated Federal commands trying to clear the Shenandoah Valley – Banks, McDowell, and, to the west, the army of John C Frémont.

As the Federal armies prepared to pursue him, Jackson

Opposite: *Troop movements in the Valley Campaign, February–June 1862.*

Right: *General Richard S Ewell led a division of Confederates in Jackson's Valley Campaign.*

Below: *Union General Frémont taking command of the Department of the West. He was removed for political and military errors but, owing to his popularity, was reassigned to western Virginia.*

withdrew gradually up the Valley (that is, to the south) with his 6000 men; Banks cautiously followed with 15,000. Then Jackson suddenly made a forced march to Swift Run Gap, in the eastern mountains. There his command was on the flank of Banks's army at Harrisonburg. Banks thus could not continue on up the Valley, for Jackson would be behind him, on the Union supply line. At Swift Run Gap in late April, Jackson was reinforced by 8000 men including the command of General Richard S Ewell; added to earlier reinforcements, this brought Rebel strength to 17,000 (which was as high as it would be in the campaign).

Of course the Federals were not standing still; Frémont began moving his forces east to join Banks in operating against Jackson. Learning of this Jackson made plans to stop that conjunction, which would likely to be fatal to his efforts. As he would so often in the future, Lee wisely gave Jackson fre rein. With a series of brilliant and lightning-quick maneuvers Jackson began his momentous campaign.

Leaving Ewell at Swift Run Gap to keep Banks in place, and sending Ashby's cavalry to make some feinting attacks, Jackson moved to strike Frémont's advance. In the most rigorous secrecy the Confederates began their march. Only Jackson knew that his destination was the town of McDowell, where R H Milroy's division was just pulling in. Driving his troops in continuous forced marches, Jackson moved to the attack. So fast did his men march that they began to be called "foot

cavalry"; they made 92 miles in four days of wet and muddy weather. On 7 May they drove Federal outposts back into McDowell. There the Federal command numbered some 6000, under Milroy and Schenck, to Jackson's 10,000. With classic skill, Jackson had maneuvered his small army to gain local superiority over his enemy.

On 8 May 1962, the Federals took the initiative at McDowell, attacking in the afternoon. Despite heavy losses, the Confederates repulsed the attack and sent the Yankees running west. Though the wet weather and enemy resistance made pursuit most difficult, the Rebels managed to chase their enemy to Franklin, West Virginia. Then Jackson withdrew, using Ashby's cavalry as a screen. The South had lost 498 men to the Union's 256, but they had won the day. Jackson, however, was by no means ready to rest. On 14 May he marched his command for Harrisonburg.

As the Confederates marched, Banks dug his army in at Strasburg and sent troops to reinforce General McDowell to the east. Thus Banks left himself with only 8000 men, a most dangerous position to be in with Stonewall Jackson around. At that point Jackson seemed, as far as the Federals were concerned, to disappear from the face of the earth. Feinting at Banks with cavalry, Jackson took the bulk of his forces east, crossed the Massanutten Mountains in the middle of the Valley, joined Ewell (making a total then of 16,000 men) and, after marching up to 30 miles a day with his "foot cavalry,"

Opposite: *The beautiful Shenandoah Valley, where Jackson pinned down a large Federal force that might otherwise have supported McClellan at Richmond.*

Left: *Belle Boyd served as a Confederate spy, reporting Union intentions in the Valley to General Jackson.*

Overleaf: *Harpers Ferry, Virginia, at the confluence of the Shenandoah and Potomac rivers. Here Jackson briefly threatened an invasion of Maryland.*

pounced on a Federal garrison of 1000 at Front Royal on 23 May.

Confederate General Richard Taylor remembered the approach to Front Royal:

Past midday . . . there rushed out of the wood to meet us a young, rather well-looking woman, afterward widely known as [Southern spy] Belle Boyd. Breathless with speed and agitation, some time elapsed before she found her voice. Then, with much volubility, she said we were near Front Royal, beyond the wood; that the town was filled with Federals, whose camp was on the west side of the river, where they had guns in position . . . that they believed Jackson to be west of Massanutten . . . that General Banks, the Federal commander, was at Winchester . . . where he was slowly concentrating his widely scattered forces to meet Jackson's advance, which was expected some days later.

Shocked by Jackson's surprise attack, the Federals at Front Royal withdrew toward Strasburg; but it was hopeless – by the end of the day the Union had lost 904 of 1063 men in the garrison, most of them captured. The Confederates had fewer than 50 casualties. Jackson had again concentrated to outnumber an outlying enemy detachment and won the day. Now he had to figure out what Banks was going to do next – stay put in Strasburg, go west to join Frémont, go north to strong positions at Winchester, or retreat east to safety near Washington. Deciding finally that Banks would probably stay put or go east, Jackson began marching to Middletown, near Strasburg.

Banks for once, did not move as expected by his enemy. After learning of the disaster at Front Royal, Banks pulled his army back to Winchester, arriving on 24 May. Hearing word of the Federal move, Jackson saw its potential for trouble – knowing the area as he did, Jackson knew the town had high ground and would be impossible to assault if the Yankees settled in. So once again, he drove his "foot cavalry" hard. At first, the exhausted Confederates dallied, wasting time looting a captured supply train, but then they marched all night and reached Winchester just after midnight.

At dawn on 25 May 1862 the Confederates drove in the Fed-

Above: *A "trooper" in Jackson's famous "foot cavalry," noted for their marching ability.*

Right: *A corps of Confederates fends off an attack from advancing Pennsylvania Bucktails in woods near Harrisonburg on 7 June 1862.*

eral pickets, and the battle of Winchester was on. For a time the Union cavalry and artillery kept the Rebels at bay; then Jackson put men on the Federal right flank, and Ewell worked his division around to the left flank. Jackson thereupon advanced his center and right together, and the Federals broke and ran. Banks withdrew under pursuit across the Potomac and out of the campaign for good. Between the defeats at Front Royal and Winchester, Banks lost some 3000 men of the 8500 in his command; Jackson's losses in the same period were about 400 of 16,000.

With these extraordinary achievements under their belts, the Confederates rested a couple of days before taking the road again. They then marched north to concentrate near Harpers Ferry. One of Jackson's opponents admiringly summarized Jackson's achievements so far:

As the result of these operations, Milroy and Schenck were now beaten, Banks's army was routed, the fertile Valley of Virginia cleared of Union troops, Harpers Ferry in danger and Maryland . . . threatened. In addition Washington was thrown into alarm and trepidation; McDowell's movement to connect with McClellan was suspended; he was ordered to move 20,000 men into the Valley to cut off Jackson, while Frémont with his whole force was ordered into the Valley at Harrisonburg for the same purpose. The whole plan of Union operations had been completely upset, and confusion reigned from

one end of the line to the other. At no time during the war was there such dismay in the North. . . . General Jackson himself seems to have been the only one who had not lost his head. He kept his army from May 26 to May 30 threatening Harpers Ferry and an invasion of Maryland.

In deciding to devote the efforts of these commands to chasing Jackson instead of reinforcing McClellan near Richmond, the Washington authorities made one of the great blunders of the conflict, quite possibly prolonging the war for three years. All this because of the brooding, brilliant Jackson and his small band of rugged soldiers.

Of course Jackson had planned everything to achieve just

that end. But his problems were by no means over. Now he had simultaneously to keep the Federals in the Valley busy, ship east the enormous quantities of supplies he had captured, and pull back from the Harpers Ferry area to avoid being trapped by the converging advances of Frémont and McDowell. Leaving the Stonewall Brigade to keep Banks in check, Jackson began pulling the rest of his forces south on 30 May. Things quickly came to a head. Jackson was riding on a railway train in front of his troops when a courier stopped the engine to tell Jackson that McDowell had recaptured Front Royal. The two Federal armies were moving in faster than expected, and Confederate forces were spread out around the Valley. Calmly Jackson issued his orders.

Left: *Colonel Turner Ashby, Jackson's cavalry commander, was killed in an engagement near Harrisonburg on 6 June.*

Below: *Virginia infantry encamped in the woods near Leesburg.*

The cavalry under Turner Ashby were sent to stop Federal's advance; an infantry detachment did likewise with McDowell's men at Front Royal. By 1 June, Jackson had pulled 15,000 men, 200 prisoners, and a double wagon-train seven miles long safely out of Strasburg; 50,000 Federals had not been able to corral them. Jackson then moved south up the Shenandoah Valley, burning bridges as he went. On 2 June Federal cavalry hit Jackson's rear guard, but Ashby delayed the Yankees long enough to give the Rebel infantry a day's lead. On 6 June came another Federal strike; this time the gallant Ashby was killed, but the Federal advance came to little – Union reinforcements could not move up because the Confederates had destroyed the bridges.

But by next day Jackson was in the worst spot of the entire campaign, squarely between two converging enemy columns. With customary boldness, he moved out to take the offensive from his position at Port Republic. On 7 June the Confederates tried without luck to draw Frémont out before McDowell arrived. Next morning a Federal detachment got into Port Republic and nearly captured Jackson – this was Shields's advance, part of McDowell's command moving up from the east. Meanwhile, Frémont moved to attack from the west. It appeared to be the end for Jackson.

Yet the Federal push became muddled, mostly due, once again, to the bridges Jackson had so carefully burned. On 8 June the Federals moved forward at Cross Keys, but were driven back and pursued; in that action Ewell's division of 6500 bested Frémont's 10,500. On the next day Jackson held Frémont at bay with Ewell and moved to attack Shields's 3000 men at Port Republic.

On the morning of 9 June the Stonewall Brigade hit the Federal right, while others attacked the enemy left. But the Confederate attacks were beaten back, and Ewell was slow to move over in support. Ewell's advance forces were then sent on an envelopment of the Federal left; this failed too, but at last the rest of Ewell's men came up. CSA General Richard Taylor remembered what happened next:

Wheeling to the right, with colors advanced, like a solid wall [the enemy] marched straight upon us. There seemed nothing left but to set our backs to the mountain and die hard. At the instant, crashing through the underwood, came Ewell, outriding staff and escort. He produced the effect of a reinforcement, and was welcomed with cheers. The line before us halted and threw forward skirmishers. A

moment later, a shell came shrieking along it, loud Confederate cheers reached our delighted ears, and Jackson, freed from his toils, rushed up like a whirlwind, the enemy in rapid retreat.

Shields and his outnumbered Federal forces retreated in good order, fighting as they went. Frémont had been unable to help due to yet another burned bridge. In two days of battle Frémont had suffered 684 casualties of 17,000 engaged; at Port Republic the Federals lost 1018. The total Southern casualties were about 1100 of 16,000 engaged. Jackson had once again defeated his enemy in detail, one division at a time. In fact, in a month of campaigning against vastly superior total Federal forces he had outnumbered his enemy in nearly every individual engagement.

With his extraordinary campaign in the Shenandoah Valley completed and the entire Federal war effort in turmoil and confusion, Jackson now marched east to join Lee in the Seven Days Battles and the Second Manassas. In one month Jackson's army had marched more than 250 miles, fought four pitched battles and endless skirmishes and had captured more than 400 prisoners and enormous quantities of arms and supplies. Jackson had brilliantly followed his own maxims of war:

Always mystify, mislead, and surprise the enemy, if possible; and when you strike and overcome him, never let up in the pursuit so long as your men have strength to follow; for an army routed, if hotly pursued, becomes panic-stricken, and can then be destroyed by half their number. The other rule is, never fight against heavy odds, if by any possible maneuvering you can hurl your own force on only a part, and that the weakest part, of your enemy and crush it. Such tactics will win every time, and a small army may thus destroy a large one in detail, and repeated victory will make it invincible.

Stonewall Jackson's tactics of speed and secrecy have been studied by military men ever since (for example, these lessons were not lost on the Nazis in preparing their *Blitzkrieg* of World War II). But the immediate effect on Southern fortunes in the Civil War was direct and profound. Jackson had played a remarkable chess game and had checkmated his enemy. Now the impetus of the war in the Eastern Theater was firmly on the Confederate side.

Right: *A Confederate camp in the Shenandoah Valley.*

On 3 September 1862 Lee proposed to Jefferson Davis that the Confederacy capitalize on its great victory at Second Manassas by mounting an immediate invasion of Maryland. In theory, there was much to recommend this bold stroke. The Union Army of the Potomac was injured and off balance, and, because a Confederate thrust into Maryland would indirectly threaten Washington, McClellan would be kept fully on the defensive and would be incapable of any meaningful counter-strokes into Virginia. Also, Lee and the South in general had high hopes that a Confederate military presence in Maryland would cause many citizens of that crucial border state to rally to the Confederate cause and perhaps even prompt the whole state to secede. Finally, and perhaps most important, a successful offensive into the North might well clinch the Confederacy's continuing efforts to gain diplomatic recognition from Great Britain and France, thus assuring the South of a badly needed infusion of foreign capital, weapons and supplies.

Attractive as all these strategic objectives were, they were predicated on some large assumptions, and indications that the assumptions may have been too large began appearing almost as soon as the Army of Northern Virginia crossed over into Maryland early in September. Marylanders did *not* hasten to throw in their lot with the CSA; indeed, they gave Lee's

army a generally chilly reception. Worse, McClellan seemed to be pulling his Union forces together remarkably efficiently and to be moving with unaccustomed dispatch toward another major confrontation.

That confrontation took place at Sharpsburg, near Antietam Creek, less than two weeks after the Maryland invasion had begun, so soon, indeed, that Lee barely had time to assemble his scattered forces to receive the shock. (But for McClellan's last-minute dawdling, Lee probably would not have had time; but then, Lee knew his dilatory opponent well.) Hostilities began early in the morning of 17 September and raged confusedly and indecisively throughout a day that would prove to be the single bloodiest in the entire Civil War. When it was over, Lee for the first time had not won a decisive victory in a major encounter. True, his army was still very much intact, but there was no denying that it had been much harmed. The number of dead, wounded and missing on each side was about the same – something over 12,000 apiece – but as a percentage of those engaged, the South's losses were much higher – on the order of 26 percent, as opposed to the Union's 16 percent.

Although the South had consistently displayed superior generalship in the battle, Antietam ended as a tactical stalemate and a strategic reversal for the Confederacy. None of the objectives of the now-stymied invasion had been achieved, and when, in the aftermath of the battle, Lincoln issued his Emancipation Proclamation, thus formally making slavery a war issue, the Confederacy's hopes of receiving foreign diplomatic recognition became even more remote, for now not even the South's best European friends wanted to appear to be on the side of slavery.

After the convulsion of Antietam the two great armies of the East rested, licking their wounds. Nonetheless, the processes of planning, raiding, and reconnaissance continued: in early October, Jeb Stuart and his Southern cavalrymen raided completely around the Army of the Potomac, as they had done before, during the Peninsular Campaign. President Lincoln goaded McClellan to action, and the general reluct-

Left: *The Battle of Antietam, 17 September 1862. Union troops crossing Burnside Bridge are met by withering Rebel fire.*

Above: *A soldier in the uniform of the Maryland Guard.*

Overleaf: *Soldiers and wagons on the bridge at Antietam Creek.*

antly put his army in motion to the south – as always, with maddening caution. Lincoln had seen it before; McClellan, Lincoln had cracked, was chronically infected with "the slows." This time, however, the president had had enough. Lincoln was not fooled into thinking Antietam a victory, as most of the North thought it. Now his general had returned to his inchworm mode of campaigning. On 7 November 1862, Lincoln removed McClellan from command. It was undoubtedly a long overdue change. But as McClellan's replacement Lincoln made a most unfortunate choice – General Ambrose E Burnside, who happened to be one of the most inept generals of all time.

A genial handsome man, Burnside sported an extravagant set of muttonchop whiskers which were perhaps his most enduring legacy – they gave the word "sideburns" to the language. Perhaps the secret of his success was that "Burn," as he was affectionately known, *looked* the way most folks thought a general should look. Favoring the appointment as well, from the president's point of view, was the fact that Burnside had no political ambitions, as McClellan certainly did (McClellan was to challenge Lincoln for the presidency in the next election). As to Burnside's generalship – Grant later wrote that he was "an officer who was generally liked and respected. He was not, however, fitted to command an army. No one knew better than himself."

When Burnside assumed command, his Army of the Potomac was near Warrenton, Virginia, nearly between Jackson's and Longstreet's divisions, Jackson then being in the Shenandoah Valley and Longstreet at Culpeper. Instead of striking

Left: *The Emancipation Proclamation, proposed five days after Antietam.*

Below: *Jeb Stuart crosses the Potomac, October 1862.*

Opposite: *The Battle of Fredericksburg, 13 December 1862. General Burnside wasted his Federal forces in frontal assaults on the entrenched enemy.*

PLAN of the BATTLE of FREDERICKSBURG

DECEMBER 13TH 1862

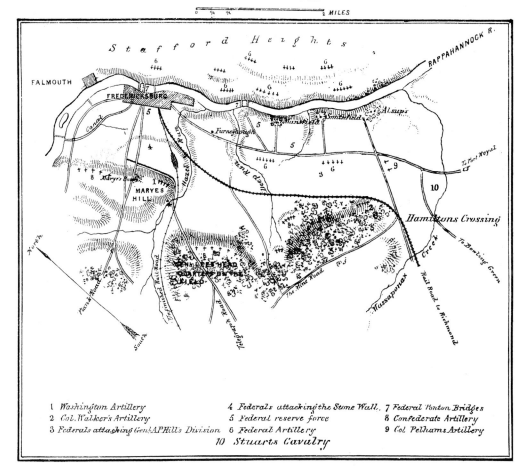

1 *Washington Artillery*   4 *Federals attacking the Stone Wall*   7 *Federal Ponton Bridges*
2 *Col. Walker's Artillery*   5 *Federal reserve force*   8 *Confederate Artillery*
3 *Federals attacking Genl. A.P.Hill's Division*   6 *Federal Artillery*   9 *Col. Pelhams Artillery*
                        10 Stuarts Cavalry

the two enemy wings in succession, with a fair chance of defeating them in detail, Burnside simply decided to try and make a beeline for Richmond, occupying Fredericksburg on the way. This was his first blunder: his real goal should have been to conquer Lee's army, not the Rebel capital.

On 17 November, Sumner's Federal division arrived across the river from Fredericksburg, which lay on the banks of the Rappahannock. At that point Sumner could have taken the town without resistance; Longstreet's division was alerted and on the way but had not yet arrived. Making his second big mistake, Burnside did not allow Sumner to cross the river but told him to wait for the arrival of a pontoon train with which to build bridges.

Longstreet arrived on 18 November; Jackson's corps did not pull in until the 30th. During this time, when the enemy was quite vulnerable, Burnside sat on the east bank waiting for his pontoons. Arriving on the 20th, Lee sized up his opponent with his usual acumen and decided to dig his army into the heights behind Fredericksburg, and from there to await

the attack. Burnside's pontoons arrived on the 25 of November; nonetheless, he delayed his offensive until 11 December, giving the Confederates time to construct virtually invulnerable positions on high ground.

Lee had wisely picked the heights behind Fredericksburg to defend rather than the town itself. Knowing he could not prevent the Federals from crossing the Rappahannock, he positioned sharpshooters in town to slow the crossing. The Confederates had 78,500 men to Burnside's 122,000 – as always, Lee was vastly outnumbered. For the Southerners, it was a matter of nearly three weeks of waiting.

On 10 December, General Burnside issued some confusing orders, the gist of which was that five pontoon bridges were to be pushed across the river for the crossing of infantry. Longstreet remembered the effectiveness of the sharpshooters Lee had placed in the town:

> On the morning of the 11th . . . the Federals came down to the river's edge and began the construction of their

Opposite top: *Union engineers placed these pontoon bridges across the Rappahannock River at Fredericksburg.*

Opposite bottom: *While some Federal troops row across the river, engineers hurry to complete a pontoon bridge.*

Right: *Union soldiers rest briefly in the center of Fredericksburg before attempting to assault the heights above the town.*

bridges, when Barksdale opened fire with such effect that they were forced to retire. Again and again they made an effort to cross, but each time they were met and repulsed by the well-directed bullets of the Mississippians. This contest lasted until 1 o'clock, when the Federals, with angry desperation, turned their whole available force of artillery on the little city, and sent down from the heights of a perfect storm of shot and shell, crushing the houses with a cyclone of fiery metal. . . . But, in the midst of all this fury, the little brigade of Mississippians clung to their work. At last, when I had everything in readiness, I sent a peremptory order to Barksdale to withdraw . . . before the Federals, who had by that time succeeded in landing a number of their troops. The Federals then constructed their pontoons without molestation, and during the night and the following day the grand division of Sumner passed over into Fredericksburg.

About a mile and a half below the town, where the Deep Run empties into the Rappahannock, General Franklin had been allowed without serious opposition to throw two pontoon-bridges on the 11th, and his grand division passed over . . . in front of Stonewall Jackson's corps. The 11th and 12th were thus spent by the Federals in crossing the river and preparing for battle.

During the night of the 12th, 50,000 Federals spent an uneasy bivouac around Fredericksburg, the time enlivened by a considerable amount of looting (though the valuables of the citizens had already been well picked over by the Confederates after the civilians evacuated to the hills and woods). Everyone knew that the next day would see a bloody contest indeed; and many Federals were already in despair at the prospect of assaulting the heights.

Longstreet wrote of the dawn of the 13th, which he observed from his position of command on the left wing of Lee's army:

As the mist rose, the Confederates saw the movement against their right near Hamilton's Crossing. [Artillery]

Major Pelham opened fire upon Franklin's command and gave him lively work, which was kept up until Jackson ordered Pelham to retire. Franklin then advanced rapidly to the hill where Jackson's troops had been stationed, filling the woods with shot as he progressed. Silently Jackson awaited the approach of the Federals until they were within good range, and then he opened a terrific fire which threw the Federals into some confusion. The enemy again massed and advanced, pressing through a gap between Archer and Lane. This broke Jackson's line and threatened very serious trouble. The Federals who had wedged themselves in through that gap came upon Gregg's brigade, and then the severe encounter ensued in which the latter general was mortally wounded. Archer and Lane very soon received reinforcements and, rallying, joined in the counter-attack and recovered their lost ground . . . the counter-attack drove the Federals back to the railroad and beyond the reach of our guns on the left. Some of our troops following up this repulse got too far out, and were in turn much discomfited when left to the enemy's superior numbers, and were obliged to retire in poor condition. A Federal brigade advancing under cover of Deep Run was discovered at this time and attacked by regiments of Pender's and Law's brigades. Jackson's second line advancing, the Federals were forced to retire. This series of demonstrations and attacks, the partial success and final discomfiture of the Federals, constitute the hostile movements between the Confederate right and the Federal left.

This fighting on the right had gone on for some three hours. Having been repulsed, Franklin's division sank into exhaustion. But while the Union assaults of the 13th were breaking on Lee's right, the other half of the Army of the Potomac had been crossing the river and gathering around Fredericksburg for an all-out offensive on Longstreet's position at and below Marye's Height. The first of six major Federal assaults set out about noon, heading straight for the strongest part of the Confederate line. Advancing across open ground, the Federal lines were torn by artillery fire, then came in rifle range of a line of Rebels, the brigade of General Thomas Cobb, posted in a sunken road behind a stone wall at the foot of Marye's Heights.

From Lee's Hill, above the battlefield, Longstreet watched wave after wave of Federal advance as if on parade to be torn to pieces at the foot of Marye's Heights:

> The field in front of Cobb was thickly strewn with the dead and dying Federals, but again they formed with desperate courage and renewed the attack and again were driven off. At each attack the slaughter was so great that by the time the third attack was repulsed, the ground was so thickly strewn with dead that the bodies seriously impeded the approach of the Federals.

And so it went as the long afternoon wore on, assault after hopeless and tragic assault, the Union dead and wounded pil-

ing higher before the stone wall. Late in the day, as the Federal efforts were tailing off on the left, Jackson ordered an advance on the right, but he was dissuaded due to extensive Federal artillery covering the open ground in his front. Lee had shifted a number of troops from his right to the center to meet the Union offensive, but they were scarcely necessary. As a Union soldier bitterly commented, "No troops in the world would have won a victory if placed in the position ours were. Few armies . . . would have stood as well as ours did. It can hardly be in human nature for men to show more valor, or generals to manifest less judgment, than were perceptible on our side that day." Another Yankee soldier put it more succinctly: "They may as well have tried to take Hell."

Night fell at last on the scene of carnage, and it was over for those Federals who had made their escape from Marye's Heights. But many were too wounded to move, or were trapped in front of enemy guns and hugging the ground all

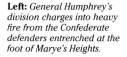

Left: *General Humphrey's division charges into heavy fire from the Confederate defenders entrenched at the foot of Marye's Heights.*

Left: *General Edwin Sumner's men launch a fruitless assault on Marye's Heights, 13 December.*

night. Union officer Joshua Chamberlain wrote an unforgettable account of that night of horror:

> Out of that silence [following] the battle's crash and roar
> rose new sounds more appalling still . . . a strange ventri-
> loquism, of which you could not locate the source . . . a
> wail so far and deep and wide, as if a thousand discords
> were flowing together into a key-note weird, unearthly,
> terrible to hear and bear . . . the writhing concord broken
> by cries for help pierced by shrieks of paroxysm; some
> begging for a drop of water; some calling on God for pity;
> and some on friendly hands to finish what the enemy had
> so horribly begun; some with delirious, dreamy voices
> murmuring loved names, as if the dearest were bending
> over them. . . .

In Burnside's tragic and stupid assaults of 13 December at
Fredericksburg the North had lost 12,700 killed and wounded
of 106,000 committed. The South's casualties were less than
half those – 5300 casualties of 72,500 engaged. During the
night a Federal prisoner caught in Confederate lines produced a memorandum from Burnside ordering renewed
attacks next day. Lee and Longstreet made ready to meet it.
The attack never came; Burnside's staff had dissuaded him.
Surveying the field that showed only dead and dying Federals
and no attack, Lee joked to Longstreet. "General, I am losing
confidence in your friend General Burnside." Perhaps Lee
should have ordered a counterattack; but he did not know

Above: *Rebel troops view ruined Fredericksburg Bridge after the battle. The defeated Union troops withdrew across the river unopposed.*

Overleaf: *Union soldiers cross the Rappahannock as engineers rush to complete a span of a pontoon bridge before Fredericksburg.*

how stricken the Federals were, and certainly he had on his
mind his army's narrow escape in the Antietam campaign.

But Burnside was not quite done yet. He made one more
effort to do his job, this time by marching the Army of the
Potomac upstream to cross the Rappahannock in hopes of
striking Lee's flank. But this operation began squarely in the
middle of the usual January thaw, with its accompanying tor-
rents of rain. During it the entire army nearly disappeared
into an apparently bottomless sea of mud. This Mud March as
history dubbed it, was soon aborted, and the bedraggled and
demoralized Army of the Potomac slogged back to their
camps across the river from Lee at Fredericksburg. A com-
passionate Longstreet wrote perhaps the best epitaph for the
Union dead.

> The spectacle that we saw upon the battle-field was one of
> the most distressing I ever witnessed. The charges had
> been desperate and bloody, but utterly hopeless. I
> thought, as I saw the Federals come again and again to
> their death, that they deserved success if courage and dar-
> ing could entitle soldiers to victory.

CHANCELLORSVILLE

Intelligence concerning enemies' doings traveled slowly and tenuously in the Civil War compared with later conflicts. But news always seemed to travel faster in the direction of Robert E Lee. The Confederate commander got his information from a variety of sources – above all from Jeb Stuart's cavalry, which were the eyes of the Army of Northern Virginia; from spies in Washington and in Southern towns occupied by the Union; from Northern prisoners and deserters; and, not infrequently, from reading Northern newspapers (there was little organized censorship in Washington, and often the South could find out about enemy operations simply by perusing the daily papers).

At the end of January, 1863, Lee learned that he had a new opponent, that the Union Army of the Potomac had seen the fourth change of command in a year. Following Burnside's debacle at Fredericksburg and his being relieved at his own request, Washington gave the army to General Joseph Hooker, called "Fighting Joe" by the press. Hooker's friends in Washington had overcome political opposition to the appointment, and Hooker was one of the few generals who genuinely wanted the job – indeed, he had schemed to get it. Lee's response to this Federal change of command is not recorded. It is likely he knew his opponent's strengths and weaknesses as well as usual. If so, Lee knew that there were two Joe Hookers: one of them an experienced, dashing and hard-fighting general; the other was a man fond of criticizing his superiors and scheming for his own benefit, and equally fond of the bottle and the ladies.

But in taking command in the winter of 1863 Hooker suddenly revealed unexpected qualities as an organizer. He repaired the Army of the Potomac from the ground up, improving the food supply, hospital care, and sanitation of his

Opposite: *General "Fighting Joe" Hooker, depicted leading his corps at Antietam, succeeded Burnside as commander of the Army of the Potomac.*

Above: *A well equipped company of Federal troops, Company H of the 36th Pennsylvania Infantry.*

Right: *The 7th New York Cavalry encamped near Washington DC.*

troops, and drilled them incessantly. The intelligence service was reorganized, with the result that there were fewer of the exaggerated estimates of Lee's strength that had plagued McClellan. The pride and morale of the army rose with its physical condition and its numbers: by April there were 122,000 men in the infantry, 12,000 men in a well-trained cavalry, and 400 cannons. Hooker called it the greatest army on the planet and crowed, "May God have mercy on General Lee, for I will have none!"

In April, Lee's Army of Northern Virginia still lay along the Rappahannock at Fredericksburg. To dislodge them, Hooker devised a plan that was sound and imaginative: leaving a force to hold Lee in position, Hooker would march the bulk of his infantry around Fredericksburg in a wide strategic envelopment, crossing the river and coming in behind Lee from the west. In theory, the Confederates then had the choice of sitting and being destroyed or retreating and thus exposing their flank to the Federals.

Opposite: *Jeb Stuart's cavalry gave Lee a reconnaissance advantage at Chancellorsville.*

Right: *The Army of the Potomac marching in force along the Rappahannock on the way to Chancellorsville.*

Below: *Hooker's troops camped between rows of breastworks in the Wilderness.*

Hooker was sure his revitalized cavalry could take on Jeb Stuart now. Thus he prepared his campaign by sending 12,000 horsemen on a raid to cut Southern supply lines in the rear. Leaving on 13 April, the Union riders soon ran into floods on the rivers that held them up for two weeks, after which they ranged around to little purpose. Lee sent Stuart and his scouts to investigate this floundering maneuver, and after receiving the report simply ignored the Federal cavalry.

On 27 April Hooker struck camp, leaving 40,000 men under General John Sedgwick to hold Lee in place at Fredericksburg, and moved the rest of his army northwest and then south across fords on the Rappahannock and Rapidan. By 30 April these forces were gathered around Chancellorsville, which was simply a wide clearing with a mansion near to a road crossing. Surrounding the clearing was the virtually impenetrable forest of the Virginia Wilderness. On the 30th the Federals began marching towards Fredericksburg, ready to take the Rebels by surprise.

However, Robert E Lee had no intention of playing his assigned role in Hooker's little game. Lee and his generals had divined what Joe Hooker was going to do almost as soon as Hooker did. A Federal general recounts the information he found in a captured officer's diary:

> In March a council of war had been held at General Stuart's headquarters, which had been attended by Generals Jackson, A P Hill, Ewell, and Stuart. They were in conference over five hours, and came to the decision that the next battle would be at or near Chancellorsville, and that the position must be prepared.

On 30 April Jeb Stuart notified Lee that Hooker was moving his army from Chancellorsville toward the Confederate rear. At that time Lee had available some 60,000 men, less than half his enemy's strength (Longstreet and Hood had gone foraging in Virginia with a large detachment). Nonetheless, Lee once again boldly split his army to meet the Federal threat. A screen force of 10,000 men under General Jubal Early was left to hold Sedgwick at Fredericksburg and was ordered to build many fires to fool the Yankees. Lee and Stonewall Jackson marched northwest on 1 May to deal with Hooker's main body.

Hooker had seen the necessity of pushing past the dense woods of the Wilderness to meet Lee on open ground, where superior Federal artillery could have room to function and the army room to maneuver. On May Day morning the Federals pulled into open country, exactly where Hooker wanted to meet the enemy. Everything was going according to Hooker's plan; Fredericksburg lay less than a dozen miles away. Then, on high ground some two miles from Chancellorsville, around ten-thirty in the morning, Federal skirmishers ran into a line of Confederate skirmishers from Anderson's and McLaws' forces. As one Union soldier recalled, "There they stood facing each other, steady and silent, gazing, the one in apparent wonderment, the other in real surprise at the unexpected situation." Soon Federal units began moving up and easily forced the Rebel skirmishers back. All that seemed necessary for the North was to form line of battle and sweep the Rebels back toward Fredericksburg.

For every Federal general confronting Robert E Lee, there came a moment of truth: when the full realization of just how

Above: *At Chancellorsville on 3 May 1863 Hooker's Union Army briefly stems a Rebel breakthrough.*

Opposite: *The last meeting of Robert E Lee with Stonewall Jackson at Chancellorsville.*

dangerous Lee was, combined with the awful responsibility of holding in his hands the future of the American nation, came down on the Union commanding officer with the force of doom itself. On 1 May, with the Wilderness at his back and commanding vastly superior forces, Hooker began to act like a beaten man at the first brush with Lee that had not been part of his pretty plan. After several hours of inactivity he fled back to the reassuring safety of the forest, overruling the furious protests of his staff and ordering all his forces back towards Chancellorsville to dig into the Wilderness. The significance of this retreat was not lost on the Union troops.

During the afternoon of 1 May Jeb Stuart's cavalry had moved freely around the Union army, and late in the day Stuart reported to Lee that the Federal right was vulnerable, "in the air," with no real protection on the flank. A Confederate officer, Robert's nephew "Fitz" Lee, recalled Lee's response:

> On May 1 General Lee wished to cut Hooker off from the United States Ford, preventing his communication with Sedgwick, and rode down himself and examined the lands all the way to the river, but found no place where he could execute this movement. Returning at night, he found Jackson and asked him if he knew of any place to attack. Jackson said he had been inquiring about roads and soon returned with the Reverend Doctor B T Lacey, who said a circuit could be made around by the Wilderness Tavern. A young man living in the country, and then in the cavalry, was sent for to act as guide. Lee and Jackson took their seats on a log to the north side of the Plank Road and a little distant from the wood. "General," Lee said, "we must get ready to attack the enemy, and you must make arrangements to move around his right flank."

The Confederates slept on the field that night. Waking in the early morning, one of Lee's staff saw an historic meeting: Jackson and Lee, finalizing their plans for yet another un-

pleasant surprise for Joe Hooker. It was to fall on that luckless Union right flank, O O Howard's XI Corps. Lee would divide forces again, holding Hooker's line of some 80,000 men in place with only 12,900 Confederates while Jackson marched 30,000 around to the west to strike the exposed Federal flank.

On the morning of 2 May 1863 the Union army was well fortified and easily handled probing attacks by the Rebels. The Federals little expected that these were feints to hold them in place; still less did they realize how thin Lee's line was in their front. Meanwhile, Jackson pulled his detachment out for the march across the front of the Union army, protected by the screen of the thick woods.

The XI Corps on the Union right was ill prepared to receive Jackson, though there had actually been fair warning of his maneuver. About noon Union general Dan Sickles had noticed Jackson's force moving to his right beyond the thick woods. Hooker, wondering at first if they were in fact headed for his right flank sent a cautionary note to Howard. But then Hooker began to convince himself that Lee must be retreating; in response to all further questions Hooker spent the afternoon insisting that the Rebels were hightailing it. When Sickles asked permission to move against the enemy column in his front, Hooker agreed, apparently figuring it would hasten the enemy in their retreat. Sickles cut his way through the brush with great difficulty and made contact with the end of the Confederate column. During the ensuing skirmish he captured some 500 men of a Georgia regiment. As these prisoners were being led to the rear, some were heard to jeer the Yanks. "You'll catch hell before night," and, "You wait until Jackson gets around to your right." (By then Jackson's column had apparently divined what their secretive commander was up to.) The Federals ignored these threats.

Left: *Stonewall Jackson's troops rout General Oliver O Howard's XI Corps.*

Below: *Generals Lee and Jackson conferring on the eye of the Battle of Chancellorsville.*

Meanwhile Hooker stripped his right flank of Barlow's division and sent them to help Sickles pursue the supposedly retreating rebels. As Sickles pulled away he left the rest of the XI Corps isolated and even more vulnerable than before.

At six o'clock in the afternoon the advance positions of the XI Corps were startled to see a mass of rabbits and deer scampering out of the woods towards them. The men whooped and laughed as the animals bolted towards the rear. There were scattered shots, and cannon suddenly appeared on the front. And then arose from thousands of throats the bone-chilling screech of the Rebel yell, and 26,000 of Stonewall Jackson's men came crashing through the Federal flank in a front a mile wide and four divisions deep, all of them shooting and screaming like demons.

Jackson's men moved straight down the enemy trenches, the 9000 men on the XI Corps fleeing in panic before them. Amidst the rout was General O O Howard, "in the middle of the roads and mounted, his maimed arm embracing a stand of colors . . . while with his sound arm he was gesticulating to the men to make a stand by their flag. With bared head he was pleading with his soldiers, literally weeping as he entreated the unheeding horde." Hooker knew nothing of the rout until he heard an aide screaming, "My God here they come!" A Union colonel remembered the appearance of the panic-stricken mob at Chancellorsville and the successful rally that followed:

It was a complete Bull Run rout. Men, horses, mules, rebel prisoners, wagons, guns, etc. etc. were coming down the road in terrible confusion, behind them an unceasing roar or musketry. We rode until we got into a mighty hot fire, and found that no one was attempting to make a stand, but every one running for his life. . . .

I found General Hooker sitting alone on his horse in front of the Chancellor House, and delivered my message; he merely said, "Very good, sir." I rode back and found the Eleventh Corps still surging up the road and still this terrible roar behind them. The rebels had received no check, but now troops began to march out on the plank road and form across it.

These troops were a division of the I Corps, whom Hooker had led forward and ordered, "Receive 'em on your bayo-

nets!" This infantry and the XII Corps artillery shoved through the fleeing men and hit the charging Rebels obliquely, slowing their advance on the left and center. Seeing a stand of Union artillery was in danger of being overrun on the right, General Alfred Pleasonton ordered Major Peter Keenan to charge his 8th Pennsylvania Cavalry into the Rebels, to buy time to turn the guns around. Keenan cheerfully accepted the order hardly knowing it was virtually suicidal. The cavalrymen, many of them scraped up from a poker game with no idea what was happening, rode directly into the middle of the oncoming enemy.

Though scores of Union saddles were emptied, the cavalry charge gave Pleasonton time to get 22 pieces aimed into the Rebels, and eventually the Federals had 36 more guns pelting the enemy from Fairview Cemetary. The Rebel advance halted before the cannonade, the troops becoming disorganized in the growing dark. Over in Hazel Grove, the 15,000 men of Sickles's III Corps had been cut off by Jackson's charge, and as night fell they began fighting their way back to

Left: *Panicked men of the Union XI Corps retreat before the onrushing Stonewall Brigade.*

Below: *Perched high in a tree, a Confederate sharpshooter takes careful aim.*

Overleaf: *Depiction of the fighting on 2 May and the wounding of Stonewall Jackson.*

their lines. After a hot and confused struggle in the gloom, with men falling from their own side's fire, part of the III Corps made it back while the rest settled into an uneasy bivouac in Hazel Grove.

Then at nine o'clock, amid the confusion of nighttime action, came the accident that was to temper this, Lee's greatest victory, with the most irreplaceable loss he had ever sustained. Stonewall Jackson had ridden out scouting from his lines just west of Chancellorsville. An officer of his staff recalled the tragedy that resulted:

> From the order Jackson sent to General Stuart it was evident that his intention was to storm the enemy's works as soon as the lines were formed. While these orders were issued, Jackson started slowly along the pike toward the enemy. When we had ridden only a few rods, our little party was fired upon [by a group of Union infantry], the balls passing diagonally across the pike. . . . At the firing our horses wheeled suddenly to the left, and General Jackson galloped away into the woods to get out of range of the bullets, but had not gone over twenty steps ere the brigade to the left of the turnpike fired a volley. It was by this fire that Jackson was wounded [by three bullets, the most serious in the left arm]. We could distinctly hear General Hill calling, at the top of his voice, to his troops to cease firing. I was alongside Jackson and saw his arm fall at his side, loosing the rein. The limb of a tree took off his cap and threw him flat on the back of his horse. I rode after him, but Jackson soon regained his seat, caught the bridle in his right hand, and turning his horse toward our men, somewhat checked his speed. I caught his horse as he reached the pike. . . .
>
> I dismounted, and seeing that he was faint, I asked the General what I could do for him, or if he felt able to ride as far as into our lines. He answered, "You had best take me down," leaning as he spoke toward me and then falling, partially fainting from loss of blood. I caught him in my arms and held him until Captain Wynn could get his feet out of the stirrups, then we carried him a few steps and laid him on the ground.

Jackson was placed on a litter, and with his bearers came under heavy artillery fire before they could reach an ambulance. That night Jackson's left arm was amputated and he began slowly to sink. Hearing the news that Jackson had been wounded by his own troops, Lee responded prophetically, "Jackson has lost his left arm but I have lost my right arm."

Also during the night, Federals bivouacking near Chancellorsville heard a strange, muffled firing. It was soon discovered, to the men's horror, that the Wilderness was burning and the woods were full of wounded; the sound was that of of exploding muskets and cartridge cases. Soldiers dashed into the woods and removed the few wounded they could reach. And then the survivors sat and listened: "Curses and yells of pain, piteous appeals and spasmodic prayers could be distinguished . . . the flames roared more fiercely, the cries grew fainter, until at last they were hushed."

Taking over Jackson's corps, Jeb Stuart rallied the men with the name of their stricken leader and led a savage attack at five in the morning of 3 May. Stuart caught the Federal III Corps in motion back toward their lines and pushed them out of high ground at Hazel Grove, whence 30 Rebel cannons were brought to bear on the heart of the Federal position at Chancellorsville. The clearing around Hooker's headquarters quickly became a maelstrom of shot and shell. Then the Rebels began shoving the Federals back toward the Rappahannock River.

That morning, 3 May, as the Confederate attack was tearing into the Union lines, Sedgwick mounted a series of assaults on Jubal Early's men outside Fredericksburg at Marye's Heights, where Burnside had been so tragically repulsed in December, and finally stormed the position with heavy losses by eleven in the morning. Sedgwick then moved toward Chancellorsville, hoping to catch Lee in a vise.

On the front porch of the Chancellor mansion, his headquarters, General Hooker seemed paralyzed amidst the furious enemy fire that was destroying his batteries one by one, smashing into the house, exploding in the upper rooms and sending showers of brick fragments flying in every direction. As he stood on the front porch leaning on a pillar, straining for the sound of Sedgwick's approach, Hooker was thrown to the ground by a shell that splintered the pillar. Dazed, he gave Couch temporary command and ordered a withdrawal to entrenchments already prepared in an arc between the Rapidan and Rappahannock. The Rebels pursued this withdrawal, their cannons firing everything they could lay their hands on – including old railroad iron, chains and tools. The woods burned again, consuming the dead and wounded of both sides.

Then Lee put the finishing touch on his masterpiece. Leaving Stuart with 25,000 men to hold Hooker's dug-in 80,000,

Lee marched with 20,000 men to confront Sedgwick's advance on his rear. Sedgwick ran into General Lafayette McLaws's troops around Salem Church on that afternoon of 3 May. By next morning Lee had surrounded Sedgwick on three sides with McLaws, R H Anderson, and Early, while also re-occupying Marye's Heights with William Barksdale's men. Sedgwick was driven back to Bank's Ford on the Rappahannock, where the Rebels harassed him strongly. The Federal division withdrew across the ford on the night of 4 May.

Lee began planning an all-out offensive against Hooker's remaining division for 6 May, an offensive that might well have been a disaster for the South given the strength of the Federal entrenchments. Concerning this plan, Confederate

General Edward P Alexander circumspectly but wryly commented, "It must be conceded that Lee never in his life took a more audacious resolve than when he determined to assault Hooker's entrenchments."

But Hooker had already had enough. Over the objections of most of his staff he withdrew across the Rappahannock during the miserably wet and muddy night of 5 May. He had gone into battle with a better than two to one advantage and had nonetheless let his forces be outnumbered in every encounter; indeed, some 30,000 Union troops had never been committed at all.

Years later, Hooker was to make a simple confession about himself at Chancellorsville, when he confronted the battlefield genius of Lee and his army: "To tell the truth, I just lost confidence in Joe Hooker."

In contrast, the morale of the Army of Northern Virginia was never so exultant, their confidence in themselves and their leaders never more unshakable. But such confidence is dangerous in armies and in leaders, as the Army of Northern Virginia was about to learn. And glorious as Lee's victory at Chancellorsville was, it was a Pyrrhic one. Casualty figures are uncertain; Lee had about 12,821 in killed, missing and wounded to Union's 17,278. But while the Federals had lost 13 percent of their army, Lee had lost 22 percent of his. Numbers were beginning to count in the war; the South's supply of manpower was limited and becoming more critical with every battle won or lost.

On 10 May Stonewall Jackson cried out in delirium from his bed, "Order A P Hill to prepare for action – pass the infantry to the front rapidly – tell Major Hawks . . ." And then, after a silence, "No, let us cross over the river and rest under the shade of the trees." On that enigmatic word of peace the great warrior died.

Left: *Southern artillery: crucial to the victory at Chancellorsville.*

Below: *Stonewall Jackson's death from wounds on 10 May saddened the South.*

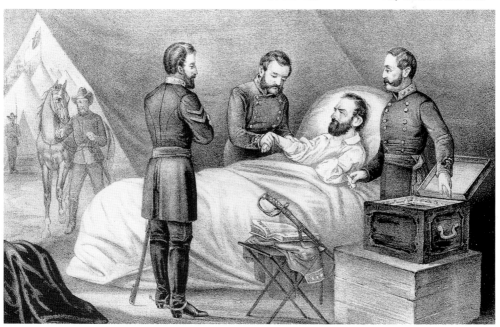

CHICKAMAUGA

As he had done in 1862 after his victory at Second Manassas, Lee proposed to follow up his triumph at Chancellorsville with a second invasion of the North. This time his target was different – Pennsylvania rather than Maryland – and his army was considerably larger and stronger than before, but the strategic considerations that suggested this move were less sanguine than those of 1862. Although the war had so far been going well for the Confederacy in the East, it was going badly in the West: the Mississippi was all but lost, and once Union General Ulysses S Grant succeeded in capturing Vicksburg, he would be free to turn his full attention on Tennessee, perhaps slashing across that state, bursting into Georgia and cutting the South in half. At the same time, the Confederacy was also not faring well on the home front. All Southern hope of foreign recognition was now dead, and the Union's ever-tightening blockade was causing mounting public privation and financial chaos.

Thus Lee's proposed second invasion of the North was as much a product of desperation as of optimism. What Lee wanted was one final, truly decisive victory in the East, one that would either win the war at a stroke or at least be so crushing as to leave his armies free to deal with the threat from the West. Some other Southern commanders, notably Longstreet, disagreed, arguing that the time to deal with the Western problem was now, and that any offensive actions that might be taken by the Union Army of the Potomac in the interim could probably be frustrated by relatively light defending forces in Virginia. How much merit Longstreet's view had is impossible to say, for it was Lee's strategy that was adopted.

The result of this great gamble was the Civil War's most famous battle and the South's most shocking defeat. In the first three days of July 1863, on and around the low hills that lie just south of the small town of Gettysburg, Pennsylvania, Lee lost a third of his army – 28,063 killed, wounded or missing. The North had not fared much better – 23,049 total casualties – but the crucial difference was that the Union could make good such losses and the Confederacy now could not. After the catastrophe of Gettysburg the South would be incapable of mounting any more important offensive operations in the Eastern Theater.

And there was good reason to suppose that the same would be true of the Western Theater as well. So far, the South had lost every major engagement fought deep within

Opposite: *Dead soldiers on the field after Gettysburg, the South's most shocking defeat.*

Right: *By the end of the third day of fighting Gettysburg was the war's costliest battle.*

Below: *Southerners attempt to breach the Union defenses at Cemetery Hill during the Battle of Gettysburg.*

its own territory, and most of these defeats had been at the hands of the tight-lipped, hard-fighting Ulysses S Grant. In a string of brilliant victories rivalling Lee's, Grant had risen from utter obscurity to fame with his operations at Shiloh, Forts Henry and Donelson, and, most of all, in the year-long campaign, extraordinary for its boldness and innovation, around the vital Mississippi River city of Vicksburg, which fell to the Union the same day as the Battle of Gettysburg concluded, 3 July 1863.

Those two Northern victories, Gettysburg and Vicksburg, were the decisive ones of the conflict, when the fortunes of war turned the corner that would lead inexorably to victory for the North. Ironically, the decisive year of 1863 had been was ushered in by the indecisive battle of Stone's River, near Murfreesboro, Tennessee. There, in three days of fighting between the Federal Army of the Cumberland and the Confederate Army of Tennessee, 20,000 men had fallen to no advantage to either side. For nearly six months thereafter

those two armies sat some 40 miles apart, waiting for their next great confrontation.

Commanding the Southern forces was General Braxton Bragg, a veteran of the Mexican War and a trusted friend of President Jefferson Davis. That friendship was not to bode well for the Confederacy. Bragg was an intelligent man but a poor leader, a great maker of plans who could not bring them to fruition.

Bragg's Federal counterpart, General William S Rosecrans, had earned his command by demonstrating a considerable talent for strategy. Early in the war Rosecrans had driven the Confederates from West Virginia, and later and been of great service to Grant in Mississippi. Rosecrans was meticulous in planning campaigns down to the last wagonwheel; he was also maddeningly slow to move. After the standoff at Stone's River, the obvious goal of his Army of the Cumberland was what was perhaps the last remaining truly vital city of the Confederacy – Chattanooga.

The city lay in the southeastern corner of Tennessee, near

Above: *General Braxton Bragg commanded the Confederate Army of Tennessee at the Battle of Chickamauga.*

Right: *The city of Chattanooga in wartime. It was an important strategic center for the South.*

the corners of Alabama and Georgia on the banks of the Tennessee River. Railroads converged on it from all over the South. For the Confederacy, Chattanooga was the best base for operations in Tennessee and Kentucky; for the North, it was the gateway to Atlanta and all of Georgia. For these reasons, Chattanooga was the real strategic center of the Confederacy. If it were to be conquered by the Union, much of the Southern war effort would be hamstrung.

In the first six months of 1863 Bragg's Confederate Army of Tennessee lay in Tullahoma, on the road between Rosecrans's army (near Murfreesboro) and Chattanooga. In May the Federal high command began to pressure Rosecrans to move against Bragg; this would not only threaten Chattanooga but would keep Bragg from sending men to reinforce Vicksburg, which was now besieged by Grant. Rosecrans waffled and Bragg did send some troops to Mississippi.

In mid-June Rosecrans finally got his army moving and at once demonstrated his strategic skills. He threatened the Rebel left flank with cavalry, and when Bragg attempted to meet this threat he discovered that two Union corps, those of George H Thomas and Thomas L Crittenden, had gotten behind the Confederate right. Confused and helpless, Bragg was forced after 30 June to pull back to his nearest stronghold – Chattanooga.

Rosecrans had made a brilliant tactical move, but then he stopped again, asking for reinforcements. These were soon available, after the fall of Vicksburg in early July. But then Washington decided to occupy conquered territory rather than reinforce Rosecrans. Meanwhile, Bragg was heavily reinforced, most notably in mid-July by General Daniel H Hill, formerly of Lee's army. Also on the way were two divisions under Longstreet, which were now available after Gettysburg. (Longstreet had suggested a move much like this well before Gettysburg).

On 5 August Rosecrans was imperatively ordered to move against Bragg. Now he faced the problem of getting the Confederates out of heavily-fortified Chattanooga. Bragg had reorganized his army to defend the city – there were two divi-

B-7043

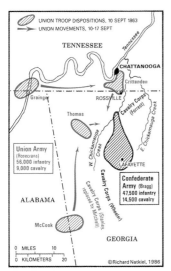

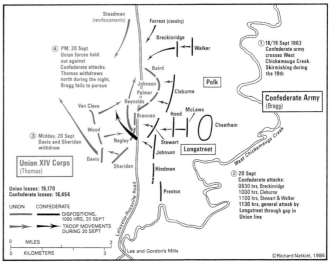

Above: *Operations in the Western Theater during September 1863.*

Below: *Union commander William S Rosecrans was a careful strategist but slow to move.*

Right: *General George Thomas (left), afterward known as the "Rock of Chickamauga," held against the Southern attack and prevented a Union rout.*

Below: *Confederate troops charge a Union line.*

sions each under Leonidas Polk, D H Hill, Simon B Buckner and W H T Walker, with cavalry under Joseph Wheeler and the brilliant Nathan Bedford Forrest (though Forrest only worked well in independent commands).

Rosecrans tried another strategic gambit, and it worked handsomely, abetted by Bragg's poor intelligence-gathering: Federal columns appeared along the Tennessee River at several widely-spaced points; as Bragg hesitated, worrying about his supply line to the rear, the Federal army crossed the river unopposed west of the city and Crittenden marched on Chattanooga.

Confronted by an enemy seeming to appear all over the map, Bragg evacuated Chattanooga on 6 September and headed south into Georgia. It was actually a wise move on Bragg's part – he was getting out of town with his army while the getting was good. Certain that they had the enemy forces on the run, the Federals made haste to pursue them into Georgia. Rosecrans boasted he would chase the Rebels to Atlanta, if not clear to the sea.

But in fact, Rosecrans was marching his army into a trap. Bragg was not fleeing; instead, he was concentrating his forces near Lafayette, Georgia, and preparing to turn and destroy the Federal army. Whether Bragg had actually planned the trap in advance is debatable. D H Hill later wrote about Bragg at that time, "The truth is, General Bragg was bewildered by 'the popping out of the rats from so many holes.' The wide dispersion of the Federal forces, and their confronting him at so many points, perplexed him, instead of being a source of congratulation that such grand opportunities were offered for crushing them one by one."

The wide dispersion Hill mentions refers to Rosecrans's deployments as he moved into Georgia – the three Union corps were spread out over 50 miles of rugged country, moving through three narrow gaps in the long ridge called Lookout Mountain. Bragg had merely to bring his superior numbers to bear and crush them in detail, one corps at a time. The Federal army was ripe for the picking.

Deliberate trap or not, Bragg and his generals proceeded to spring it ineptly. The forces of General Leonidas Polk were ordered to attack Thomas on 10 September. Though Polk's men appeared in Thomas's path, nothing happened. Another attack failed to materialize on the 11th. Two days later Bragg

arrived at Chickamauga Creek, expecting Polk to have anni-
hilated Crittenden's corps there. Polk had not budged.

The continuing presence of parties of Confederates in his
front, all of whom seemed to be withdrawing towards
Lafayette, finally tipped off Rosecrans that he was in serious
trouble. On 12 September he urgently ordered his wings to
converge toward the center and concentrate on the west side
of Chickamauga Creek, near Lafayette. Bragg, meanwhile,
was also concentrating his forces near the creek and was im-
patiently awaiting the arrival of Longstreet's divisions. When
they arrived Bragg would have over 65,000 men to Rosecrans's less than 60,000.

Rosecrans had divined what Bragg's strategy would be in
the battle, which was to move around the Union left and cut
off their line of retreat – road to Chattanooga. The Federal
commander thus paid special attention to his left, placing
General George H Thomas in command there. The posi-
tioning of the indomitable Thomas was to prove a decision
most fortunate indeed for the fate of the Union army.

On the night of the 18th both sides prepared for battle,
Rosecrans building a strong defensive position. Because of
the thick woods in the area, neither general knew where his
enemy was – or, indeed, where his own forces were. Bragg
thought the Union left was at Lee's and Gordon's Mill, and
planned his attack to flank that position and gain the road to
Chattanooga. Since Rosecrans had anticipated that, he had
strung his lines out north from the mill and along the road. By
daybreak on 19 September Thomas had formed his line of
battle above the steep sides of Horseshoe Ridge.

As dawn came on the 19th, both armies were poised for
battle at Chickamauga Creek. Prophetically, the creek's name

came from an old Cherokee Indian word meaning "River of
Death."

The battle began by accident. Unsure whether there were
Confederates north of the creek, Thomas sent cavalry to
scout his front. Soon these men stumbled on some of Forrest's cavalrymen, who were dismounted on the Reed's
Bridge road. The Southerners retreated under fire back to
their infantry, who then pushed forward. Slowly the battle
spread outward until both armies were firing all along the
line. There followed a confused but nonetheless bloody day
of fighting. As Hill later wrote, "it was the sparring of the
amateur boxer, and not the crushing blows of the trained
pugilist." All morning there was a gap of some two miles in
the Federal lines, but it was hours before Bragg found the gap
and tried to exploit. Finally, an attempt was made by the
forces of John B Hood, whose division of Longstreet's command had just arrived ahead of the others. Hood smashed the
right center of the Union line and got on to the Chattanooga
road, but a wave of Federals charged in to drive them back.

After a day of heavy but indecisive fighting on 19 September the guns fell silent in the late afternoon. By then Longstreet had arrived by rail with the rest of his forces. It took
him until eleven at night to find Bragg, who got out of bed for
a conference. Dividing his army into two wings, Bragg gave
the right to Polk and the left to Longstreet. Polk was to begin
at dawn with a strong assault on Thomas; after Polk's attack
there were to be successive attacks down the line to the
south. As the Confederate general spoke they heard the
sound of axes from the Federal lines – the Army of the Cumberland was building a strong defensive line of log breastworks through the thick woods.

At dawn on the 20th visibility was negligible due to the woods and a thick blanket of fog. Bragg sat in his head-quarters straining to hear the sound of Polk's dawn attack. After an hour of inactivity a messenger was dispatched to find Polk. The general was discovered reading a newspaper on a farmhouse porch while waiting for his breakfast. When queried about his attack, Polk grandly responded, "Do tell General Bragg that my heart is overflowing with anxiety for the attack – overflowing with anxiety, sir!" When this was reported at about nine-thirty to Bragg, he swore, "in a manner that would have powerfully assisted a mule team in getting up a mountain," and ordered Polk to begin the attack on Thomas immediately.

By this time the front stretched some two miles, north to south, Polk's men fell with a will onto Thomas, who held on to his breastworks in the Horseshoe Ridge but soon found his more vulnerable left flank being pushed across the vital road to Chattanooga. Again and again Thomas called for reinforcements from Rosecrans, to whom he had a direct telegraph wire (one of the first of these on any battlefield). Confusion began to creep into Union deployments due to the thick woods. At eleven in the morning this confusion created a strange and catastrophic turn in the battle. An aide, who had been riding behind the Union position, reported to Rosecrans that there was a gap in the Federal line between T J Wood's and J J Reynolds's divisions. Intending to seal that gap, Rosecrans hurriedly sent an order to Wood to move left, to "close up on and support" Reynolds (both these divisions lay near the Federal right flank, which was so far inactive).

But the aide had made a disastrous mistake: there was no gap in the Union line. Between Wood and Reynolds was John Brannan's division, exactly where they were supposed to be, but so hidden by the woods that the aide had not seen them.

Wood received Rosecrans's order and puzzled over it. How was he to "close up on and support" Reynolds when Brannan

was between them? Finally Wood decided that "support" was the operative idea and ordered his division to pull out of line and march behind Brannan towards Reynolds. His men formed line of march and headed for the rear, leaving a gaping hole in the Union right wing.

At just that moment, hardly a stone's throw away but still hidden in the woods, Longstreet was massing eight brigades for the attack. (That the attack was gathering then and there was apparently sheer coincidence.) At the head of the column rode hard-fighting John B Hood. About eleven-thirty

Opposite: *A Rebel attempt to take a Union battery at Chickamauga is foiled by Lieutenant Van Pelt and his men.*

Right: *Confederate General John Bell Hood.*

Below: *Southern marksmen in the Chickamauga woods.*

in the morning the Confederates headed for the Union lines and found to their astonishment that no one was there.

The results were immediate and dramatic. A solid column of screaming Rebels flooded straight through the Union line, crashed on to the end of Wood's departing column, and scatted the divisions of Federal generals Philip Sheridan and Jefferson C Davis, who had begun moving into the gap from the right. Hood, having lost the use of an arm at Gettysburg, was wounded seriously in the leg, but his men pushed on.

During this rout the Federals lost thousands in casualties and captured; Hill later wrote that he had never seen Federal dead so thickly blanketing the ground except after the suicidal charge at Fredericksburg. Among the fleeing were a panicky and demoralized Rosecrans and most of his staff. Assuming his whole army was routed, Rosecrans ordered everyone to retreat to Chattanooga.

Fortunately for the Union, not everyone obeyed that order, because Rosecrans was wrong about his forces being totally beaten. Along Horseshoe Ridge, to the left, Thomas was holding on like grim death, with thousands of enemy swarming

Left: *The fight at Orchard Knob, one of a number of battles near Chattanooga in November 1863.*

Above: *Ulysses Grant, the new Union commander, views the fighting at Chattanooga.*

danger. Yet not all the routed Federal divisions had continued on to Chattanooga. Wood, Brannan and Reynolds fell into position on Thomas's right, Wood meeting the first appearance of Longstreet's men with a determined bayonet charge that stopped the Rebels in their tracks. As Thomas's line on the right stabilized a little, Rebel assaults swarmed on to his left flank. D H Hill later wrote admiringly of Thomas's stand, "that indomitable Virginia soldier, George H Thomas, was there and was destined to save the Union army from total rout and ruin, by confronting with invincible pluck the forces of his friend and captain [Bragg] in the Mexican War."

As the afternoon wore on Thomas's Federals were running out of ammunition, their front and flanks were staggering under heavy assaults, and the enemy was moving around the right flank to the rear. Rebel cannons were moving into position to enfilade the Union right, and there were no men left to do anything about it. And then, at three-thirty, Thomas noticed a column of dust approaching in his rear. If the troops that were making that dust were foe, his men were doomed. An officer was dispatched to take a look. They proved to be friends, part of two divisions of reserves commanded by General Gordon Granger, who had just committed a serious and most salutary breach of orders. Placed in reserve by Rosecrans, with strict orders to guard the road to Chattanooga, Granger had listened with increasing anxiety to the sound of battle growing steadily on the Federal left. Finally, he made his own decision – "I am going to Thomas, orders or no orders." By four o'clock Granger was shaking hands with an overjoyed Thomas, men and ammunition arriving rapidly behind them. Granger's men cleared the enemy from a valley in the rear, and a path of retreat was at last open.

The South had won the field at Chickamauga, one of the greatest victories of the war in the Western Theater. But General George Thomas had saved the Federal army to fight another day, becoming in the process one of the immortal heroes of the Union cause. To history, Thomas is forever "The Rock of Chickamauga."

Casualties in the battle were among the worst of the war: of 66,326 Southerners engaged, there were 2312 killed, 14,674 wounded, 1468 missing, a total of 18,454 casualties; for the North, of 58,222 engaged, there were 1657 killed, 9756 wounded, 4757 missing, a total of 16,170. Altogether, nearly 35,000 men fell; both sides had lost 28 percent of their forces.

Back in his headquarters, Bragg could not seem to get it

around the steep sides of the ridge. At Confederate headquarters Longstreet was begging General Bragg to give him all his remaining troops to surround Thomas's position. Bragg, seemingly of the opinion that his army was losing, replied that the rest of the men had "no fight left in them." Having fought at the side of Lee most of the war, Longstreet's frustration with the obtuse Bragg must have been titanic.

By mid-afternoon Thomas was watching enemy forces moving towards his right. He knew his front along the precipitous slopes was strong, but his flanks were in great

Left: *An N C Wyeth portrait of General Grant. His arrival at Chattanooga transformed an impending Union disaster into a successful offensive.*

Opposite top: *Confederate General John B Hood is wounded at Chickamauga. He lost his right leg.*

Opposite bottom: *General Thomas's men repel a Rebel charge at Chickamauga.*

into his head that he had won. His generals pressed him to pursue, the impetuous Forrest screaming at his commander, "You are a coward and a damned scoundrel!" By next morning, 21 September, Bragg was finally willing to admit victory. He sent a force to Missionary Ridge in Chattanooga with orders to attack; but Bragg's men found the Federals "ready to receive and entertain us."

Yet Bragg had one more chance to reclaim Chattanooga. He put his army in strong position on the ridges and settled in to starve the Yankees out. The Federal army was now besieged deep in enemy territory. And starve the Yankees did, while both Bragg and Rosecrans spent their time writing elaborate reports blaming their subordinates for everything.

On 23 October 1863 General Ulysses S Grant arrived in Chattanooga. He had been appointed to command of most Union forces west of the Alleghenies. His first act was to replace the spent Rosecrans with Thomas as commander of the Army of the Cumberland. Gaining reinforcements, Grant soon had food and supplies flowing into the city. And on 25

November the vindictive Federals, shouting "Chickamauga!" as they charged, swarmed up and over the slopes of Missionary Ridge and chased the Confederate Army of Tennessee back to Georgia in one of the worst routs the Confederacy ever suffered. Chattanooga, the strategic center of the South, was secure for the Union. Now the way was prepared for William Tecumseh Sherman's devastating march across Georgia to the sea.

Contemplating this last golden opportunity lost, General D H Hill later concluded:

It seems to me that the *élan* of the Southern soldier was never seen after Chickamauga – that brilliant dash which had distinguished him was gone forever. He was too intelligent not to know that the cutting in two of Georgia meant death to all his hopes . . . He fought stoutly to the last, but, after Chickamauga, with the sullenness of despair and without the enthusiasm of hope. That "barren victory" sealed the fate of the Southern Confederacy.

EPILOGUE: THE END OF THE CONFEDERACY

When, at the end of 1863, Ulysses S Grant lifted the siege of Chattanooga, the Union was at last in a position to begin its invasion of the Deep South. But the anticipated lunge into Georgia did not start immediately. Early in the new year Grant was recalled to Washington, where he was created lieutenant general (a rank held previously only by George Washington), placed in charge of all the Union armies and given the task of devising a strategy for winning the war. When it emerged, that strategy, in essence, involved not one invasion but two: the thrust into Georgia, to be commanded by Sherman, would be coordinated with a simultaneous drive south from Washington aimed at Richmond – this latter operation to be conducted by General George Meade under Grant's personal supervision.

Both offensives began on the night of 3-4 May 1864. Within two days, Grant's part of the operation had become embroiled in savage fighting with Lee's Army of Northern Virginia, and this continued almost unabated for the next six weeks. Time and again – in The Wilderness, at Spotsylvania, at North Anna and at Cold Harbor – Lee attempted to block Grant's advance, and each time, after a bloody confrontation, Grant would disengage, swing around to the east and continue his relentless drive southward. By 18 June Grant was actually south of Richmond, facing Lee's strongly fortified position at Petersburg. At this point Grant abandoned maneuver and settled in for a long siege, reasoning that since Petersburg was the most important rail junction supplying Richmond, it was as good a place as any to begin starving the Rebel capital into submission. It was also a good – perhaps necessary – place to pause and try to recover from the rigors of the campaign thus far. The casualties on both sides had been appalling: 50,000 (41 percent) for the Union and 32,000 (46 percent) for the Confederacy. Given Lee's lack of reserve manpower, the figures were more ominous for the South than even the numbers and percentages might suggest.

Meanwhile, Sherman, fighting all the way, slowly made his

Above: *Remains of a Confederate battle flag. Many Southern units refused to surrender their banners but burned, buried, or hid them.*

Left: *Richmond, burned by Rebel soldiers as they prepared to abandon the Southern capital.*

Opposite: *A Union mortar battery prepares its position. Such siege weapons represent the North's overwhelming military strength.*

way towards Atlanta. He invested the Georgia capital in July, finally captured it in September and, after burning much of it, left it on 15 November to begin his infamous march to Savannah and the sea. Leaving a 60-mile-wide swath of calculated destruction in his wake, he reached and took Savannah on 21 December. A few days earlier, Union General George Thomas, the "Rock of Chickamauga," had, on Sherman's orders, engaged and all but destroyed the army of Confederate General John Bell Hood in Tennessee. There was now hardly any major military organization left in the Confederacy that might be sent to reinforce Lee at Petersburg.

By early 1865 it was obvious to all that the end was near. Sherman had wheeled north into the Carolina, and there seemed little hope that a hastily-improvised Confederate force under Joseph E Johnston could long deter Sherman from his ultimate objective: junction with Grant outside Petersburg. There were no great battles left to the Confederacy now, only the slow agony of failing strength and hope in the trenches of Petersburg. On 2 April 1865, after six months of devastating siege, Lee and the remains of his army bolted from Petersburg. Lee was making a last desperate effort to join forces with Johnston's army in South Carolina, but his leaving doomed Richmond. Lee was run to ground by Grant and General Philip Sheridan, who circled and harried the pathetic remains of the Army of Northern Virginia until that 9 April at Appomattox when Lee's men made their last charge, breaking through the center of Sheridan's line as it blocked their path. For a brief moment there was open country in front of the Army of Northern Virginia. Then from over a hill appeared Union infantry, line after line of blue, marching to fill that last gateway to freedom. Soon from

within Confederate lines came a rider carrying a white flag into the ranks of the enemy.

The war was over. Lee's surrender to Grant at Appomattox on 9 April 1865 largely ended the hostilities (Johnston surrendered to Sherman on the 8th). Now the country was one again, the glorious exploits of the men in gray a matter of history and proud memory.

Throughout the long days of the war a volunteer nurse in Union military hospitals had put into impassioned words this thoughts about the struggle. He was Walt Whitman, later to be recognized as the great poet of the reborn nation. At the war's conclusion, Whitman wrote this benediction:

The dead in this war – there they lie, strewing the fields and woods and valleys and battlefields of the South: Virginia, the Peninsula, Malvern Hill and Fair Oaks, the banks of the Chickahominy, the terraces of Fredericksburg, Antietam bridge, the grisly ravines of Manassas, the bloody promenade of the Wilderness.

The dead, the dead, the dead . . . somewhere they crawled to die, alone, in bushes, low gullies, or on the sides of hills . . . Our young men once so handsome and so joyous, taken from us . . . the clusters of camp graves . . . the single graves left in the woods or by the roadside . . . the general million, and the special cemeteries in almost all the states.

The infinite dead, the land entire saturated, perfumed with their impalpable ashes' exhalation in Nature's chemistry distilled; and shall be so forever in every future grain of wheat and ear of corn, and every flower that grows, and every breath we draw.

Opposite: *A Union soldier surveys a ruined Richmond and its still-standing Southern capitol.*

Right: *Union soldiers at Appomattox Court House pose after the surrender ceremony.*

Below: *Grant and others (Sheridan between Grant and Lee, Meade at Grant's left) with General Lee at the McLean house at Appomattox Court House on 9 April 1865.*

Northern Victories

THE NORTH GOES TO WAR

The Civil War arose from a complex of problems – political, philosophical, economic and moral – that had haunted the United States from the beginning, implicitly from their first days as colonies and explicitly from their inception as a nation. These problems rolled through the years of the nineteenth century, gaining momentum, swelling until they had grown beyond the control of even the wisest of people.

Chief among these problems – or at least the one that proved to be breaking point – was the institution of human slavery imposed upon black people (which endured in America longer than in any other Western nation). By the mid-nineteenth century, slavery had been eliminated throughout the North, but was maintained in the South with a tenacity that was only partially explainable by slavery's support of the cotton economy. The other major problem festering over the years was that of federalism versus states' rights: federalism, strongest in the North, proclaimed the primacy of the Federal Government; states' rights doctrine, dominant in the South, upheld the primacy of each state's government.

These and related problems had tended increasingly to split the country along sectional lines. So it was that in the early spring of 1861 the volatile spirit of sectionalism came to its long-feared explosion point: when the wisest of people cannot solve a nation's problems, they must often be solved by the strongest, and great suffering results.

In the midst of this crisis, the most serious in the nation's

Left: *Lincoln as portrayed by Alexander Gardner, an associate of Mathew Brady. Lincoln's first priority in conducting the Civil War was restoration of the Union. Emancipation of the slaves came second.*

Previous page: *The Battle of Gettysburg.*

Opposite top: *Philadelphia Zouaves parade past Independence Hall. Anticipating a short war, Northern volunteers flocked to join locally-raised army companies.*

Opposite bottom: *Lincoln's call for the raising of a militia to suppress the insurrection in South Carolina impelled thousands to volunteer for the fight. Northern enthusiasm was typified by this fanciful painting of joyful Uncle Sams marching into Dixie.*

PHILADELPHIA ZOUAVE CORPS.

history, the man whose election helped to precipitate it was inaugurated president. Elected by less than 50 percent of the voters, Abraham Lincoln came to the White House largely untried in national politics – an unknown quantity. Even before he arrived in Washington in February 1861, Lincoln faced the prospect of dealing with a rival government that was already claiming all Federal property within the boundaries of seven Southern states – South Carolina, Mississippi, Florida, Alabama, Georgia, Louisiana and Texas. After the November 1860 election these states had seceded from the Union and now called themselves the Confederate States of America. They had assembled their own representatives, who drew up a Constitution and selected a president – Jefferson Davis, a former secretary of war in Washington. In his first inaugural address Lincoln repudiated the Confederate claim, vowing to "hold, occupy, and possess" all Federal property. He made it clear that secession would not be tolerated.

Most significant among the Federal properties claimed by the Confederates were symbols of Federal power: four garrisons – three in Florida, far from the centers of government, and one in South Carolina. By the end of 1860, the attention of the entire country was riveted on the last garrison – Fort Sumter, in Charleston Harbor. As early as 26 December 1860 the Federal commander there, Major Robert Anderson, had withdrawn troops from the even more vulnerable Fort Moultrie, also in the harbor, and moved them to Sumter. At the beginning of 1861 this garrison, a pentagonal fort occupying an artificial island just off-shore, was unfinished, poorly

armed, understaffed and running low on food. In January a provision boat sent by then President Buchanan had been fired on and turned back. Since then the Confederates had erected a semicircle of batteries on the mainland and islands around the fort. The Federals inside had done what they could to prepare for battle.

Both Secretary of State Seward and aging general-in-chief Winfield Scott pressed Lincoln to evacuate Sumter. The President decided on 29 March 1861 neither to evacuate nor to reinforce the garrison, but to send a ship with provisions for the soldiers. On April 6 Lincoln advised South Carolina's governor of this order; he was making sure that the next critical step, an act of aggression, would have to be taken by the South.

On the next day the Confederate commander in Charleston, General P G T Beauregard, cut off communications between Charleston and Sumter. Events accelerated, pulled on by the seemingly irresistible magnet of war. On 8 April the Confederacy organized its forces in the harbor. Two days later Beauregard was instructed by the Confederate Government to demand the fort's surrender and evacuation; the demand was presented to Major Anderson on 11 April. Anderson replied that he would evacuate on 15 April unless he were attacked or received further orders from Washington. This last stipulation did not satisfy the Confederates.

At 3:20 in the morning on 12 April, Anderson received a note from Beauregard's messengers: "We have the honor to notify you that we will open the fire . . . in one hour from this time." Sumter's commander notified Captain Abner Doubleday (later to become incorrectly known as the founder of modern baseball) that the attack would begin at first light and that to conserve ammunition, fire should not be returned until broad daylight. After giving his final notice to Major Anderson, General Beauregard sent firing orders to Captain G S James in Fort Johnson, on James Island. Captain James

offered a friend the "honor" of discharging the opening shot; the friend agitated, replied, "I could not fire the first gun of the war." At 4:30 AM, 12 April, Captain James himself pulled the lanyard.

Fort Sumter, indefensible at the outset, endured 34 hours of bombardment and some 4000 shells: there was clearly little point in continued resistance. It was agreed that the Federals would evacuate the fort on 14 April, and that they might salute their flag with 100 guns before leaving. During this salute some sparks from the smoldering fires accidentally ignited a cannon cartridge as it was being loaded; the resulting explosion killed Private Daniel Hough instantly and seriously wounded five others, one of whom died. In this pointless accident fell the first soldiers of the war.

After their salute the Federals marched out, banners flying, the band playing "Yankee Doodle," and sailed off on the steamer *Baltic* to a heroes' welcome in New York. Confederate forces marched into the fort with equal ceremony. Maybe that's how it will be, many Southerners thought: we shell them a little and they go away. Maybe it would all be this easy: the North would soon be compelled to recognize the military superiority of the South and, lacking the South's will to fight, would sue for peace. Thus, without too much pain, would the South win its independence.

But the South did not yet know the resolve of Abraham Lincoln. On 15 April the president declared a state of "insurrection" and called for 75,000 volunteers to join the regular army in suppressing it. Northern States were immediately suppor-

Below left: *US recruiting poster. As the war drew on, ever more volunteers were needed.*

Below: *Wives and children bid farewell to the men of the Union garrison at Fort Sumter.*

Above: *Rebel batteries shelling Fort Sumter on 13 April 1861. The fort was evacuated the next day.*

Below: *Southern dignitaries view the defenses at Fort Sumter a few days after it fell to Rebel bombardment.*

tive, Border States resistant. On 19 April Lincoln declared a blockade of all Confederate ports. In the wake of Sumter four more states seceded – Virginia, Arkansas, Tennessee and North Carolina – but the Border States – Delaware, Maryland, Kentucky and Missouri – stayed loyal. Six days after Sumter fell, US Army General Robert E Lee declined an offer to command Union forces, resigned his commission and proclaimed his duty to defend his home state of Virginia.

Thus the war began. Everywhere citizens rallied to the colors, galvanised by romantic visions of a noble cause, of heroic battle. But a few, above all Abraham Lincoln, already understood that the coming conflict would be long and bitter. On paper, the North seemed to have some obvious advantages: it was more than twice as populous as the South, had built an industrial plant five times as large, and possessed a much superior system of communications, a far more flexible agricultural base, and considerably more ready cash. But the South had one unquantifiable advantage that would, during the first half of the war, prove nearly decisive: a seemingly inexhaustible reservoir of great commanders – Lee, Jackson, Stuart, Longstreet, Forrest, the two Johnstons, and many more. Against such men, the Northern mediocrities of early years of the war, generals such as McDowell, McClellan, Pope, Hooker, and Burnside, could only come to grief.

Yet even as the furnace of war was slowly hardening the rank and file of the Union armies, so it was also burning away the dross in the Federal officer corps, revealing hitherto-unrecognized talent. When the new breed of Northern commanders finally emerged – men such as Grant, Sherman, Sheridan, Thomas, and Meade – they differed from their Southern counterparts in important ways. They were less interested in (and propably less adept at) classical tactics, but they displayed a truly formidable grasp of strategy. They seemed to understand that this was a new kind of conflict, a Total War, and they were perhaps psychologically better prepared than their enemies to do whatever was necessary to win it. Their great victories – Gettysburg, Vicksburg, Atlanta, Petersburg, and the rest – were sometimes appallingly costly and seldom elegant, but in sum they were devastating.

SHILOH

In April of 1862 the war was a year old, and the original optimistic hopes on both sides for a short conflict, resolved in one or two decisive battles, were fading. After the fall of Fort Sumter, Lincoln had called for three-month volunteers to put down the rebellion. That was expected to be time enough. But the initial major battle of the war, the First Bull Run (Virginia) in July 1861, had been a humiliation for the Union, as had the action as Ball's Bluff, Virginia, in October.

Far left: *General William Tecumseh Sherman distinguished himself at Shiloh, the first battle in the Western Hemisphere to involve more than 100,000 men.*

Left: *Disposition of the forces at Shiloh on 5 April 1861.*

Below: *The engagements on the first and second days.*

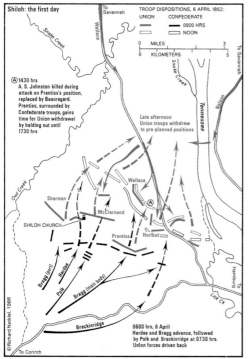

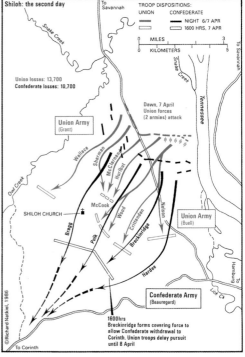

It began to be clear that in order to defeat the South, the North had to invade and occupy it. If the North could be said at this stage to have a strategy to achieve that gargantuan task, it was to split the Confederacy on a north-south line along the Mississippi River, then east-west somewhere through the middle of the south; then it would deal with the fragments. To achieve the north-south sundering, Federal forces early in 1862 began moving south into Rebel territory from Kentucky, along the Cumberland and Tennessee rivers.

The district commander of these forces was an up-and-coming Union general named Ulysses S Grant. In February 1862 Grant had leaped from obscurity into national prominence with his dramatic campaigns to capture Forts Henry and Donelson. His surrender note to the latter – "No terms except for immediate and unconditional surrender can be accepted" – had earned him the nickname "Unconditional Surrender" Grant.

But no one really knew yet what Grant was capable of. He was an unkempt and not particularly soldierly looking man whose gait was a sort of controlled stumble. His habitual expression was once described in the words "He looked as if he had decided to drive his head through a brick wall and was about to do it." There was talk, perhaps more than rumor, about his past – failures in business, a near-court-martial in his first military command some years before and a fondness for the bottle abnormal even for an officer. And after his recent victories Grant had somehow displeased his superiors enough to get himself relieved of command and virtually under arrest for a week. He was no one's image of a great commander.

Right: *The notoriously unkempt General Ulysses S Grant, the Union's finest commander.*

Overleaf: *Scouts and guides of the Union army. Poor Northern intelligence-gathering led to Grant's inadequate preparation against the first Confederate attack at Shiloh.*

When Grant got back his district command on 13 March, he found his army on the Tennessee River, part at the small town of Savannah, Tennessee, and part nine miles above, on the western bank of the river near Pittsburg Landing, Tennessee. His plan was to concentrate these forces, called the Union Army of the Mississippi, with those of General Don Carlos Buell's Army of the Ohio; the latter were ordered to move southwest from Nashville. When finally combined, the two armies were to move on Corinth, Mississippi, an important Confederate rail center (all these towns were near the conjoined corners of Tennessee, Mississippi and Alabama). Buell began promptly to move his forces, but then was held up for ten days by floods.

Grant knew there were enemy forces near his camps and a large Rebel force in Corinth. He did not know, however, that they were preparing an offensive designed to smash his army before Buell could reach him. (As was often the case during the war, Southern intelligence-gathering was more accurate than that of the North.) For the purpose of dealing with Grant's forces, General P G T Beauregard, the hero of Sumter and Bull Run, had assembled in Corinth a new Confederate Army of 40,000 men, consisting of corps under Generals Leonidas Polk, Braxton Bragg, William J Hardee, and John C Breckenridge. In overall command of this new Confederate Army of the Mississippi was General Albert Sidney Johnston, considered among the greatest hopes of the southern cause.

Johnston developed a bold offensive strategy, overruling Beauregard's insistence on a defensive approach. According to the plan, the Confederate Army was to move out of Corinth, envelop the Union left flank by the river – thus cutting off reinforcements from Buell in the east – and push the Federals back to Owl Creek to the northeast, thereby forcing a surrender.

On 6 April Grant had six divisions – those of John A McClernand, William H Wallace, Lew Wallace (later the writer of *Ben Hur*), Steven A Hurlbut, William Tecumseh Sherman and Benjamin M Prentiss – encamped on the west side of the Tennessee River in the vicinity of Pittsburg Landing and the little log meetinghouse called Shiloh Church. A considerable portion of these 33,000 troops were quite green; indeed, many scarcely knew how to load their rifles, and some of the officers were little more experienced.

Though there had been continuous skirmishing along his front for some days, Grant wrote his superior Halleck on 5 April, "I scarcely have the faintest idea of an attack . . . being made on us." Grant's close associate, Sherman, concurred with this supposition: they reasoned that Corinth was a good defensive position and that the Confederates would not venture out of it. The Union camps were therefore chosen for their comfort rather than for their defensive strength; guarding was desultory, and there were no entrenchments.

On the morning of 6 April Grant confidently left his camp

well before dawn to have breakfast in Savannah and meet with Buell, who had arrived there the day before. Grant was on crutches, lamed by a riding accident. Most of his troops were beginning a normal day, having a leisurely breakfast and polishing up for the usual Sunday inspection.

Then, still before dawn, the Rebel attack swarmed into the Union camps with overpowering suddenness and strength. Companies of the 16th Wisconsin and 21st Missouri were sent to reinforce the slim Union forces in the front, but these were soon driven back. The majority of the 25th Missouri (on the left middle of the Union lines) were standing at rest in their camp when they were astonished to see a huge body of Confederates, line after line, unpreceded by skirmishers, coming down a slope toward them within easy range. Both sides simply stood and fired away, with devastating effect – at this point in the war, many considered it cowardly to dig a hole or even to take cover.

Meanwhile, at six o'clock that morning, Hildebrand's hastily-formed brigade of Sherman's division, on the right of the Union lines, received the full force of the Confederate attack. Green troops of the 53rd Ohio immediately broke and ran, followed by two other regiments. The rest of Sherman's division fell back from their camps after some resistance, and by eight in the morning Prentiss's whole division had done likewise, pursued through their camps and across a ravine.

About that same hour, Confederate General Johnston's designs on the left flank of the Federal army – the original focal point of his strategy of envelopment – began to take shape. On the extreme Union left was a small brigade of Sherman's division, without artillery, led by Colonel David Stuart. His small force met a strong charge by the Rebels and, after some initial panic, was formed into line and mounted a furious resistance some 500 yards behind their original position. This Union stand, coming as it did after a frightened stampede,

was so determined that it convinced the enemy it must be a trap: as one Rebel officer observed, "No such little body of men could ever stand up and fight like that without something back of them." Stuart's brigade would hold on until after two o'clock that afternoon, withdrawing only when its ammunition was exhausted. The wary Confederates, still suspecting a trap and not realizing how small a force had stayed them, did not immediately press their advantage.

By midmorning the fighting was furious all along the line. The battle clearly had the appearance of a major Confederate victory. Most of the Union forces had pulled back from their camps with heavy losses. There was a serious gap in the center of the Federal line, and hordes of Union stragglers were collecting along the river to the rear. The raw volunteers of the Northern armies had experienced their baptism of fire.

Things were indeed going well enough for the Confederacy on the morning of 6 April, but not so well as they seemed to the Rebels. Johnston's attack was in fact poorly organized: his units had intermingled, the commands becoming confused; men were thrown into attack by columns as they arrived on the roads, and no reserves were left at all; the main thrust of Johnston's original attack plan, the left of the Union line, had bogged down. Instead of the intended envelopment, there was a disorderly advance all along the front.

Furthermore, Union forces were withdrawing not in disarray but in rather good order, the stragglers notwithstanding. Having heard the onset of hostilities that morning, Grant rushed to Pittsburg Landing from Savannah, arriving about eight o'clock. Not having had time to see Buell in Savannah, Grant sent a note to hurry him along. Lew Wallace was ordered to rush his 5000 troops south from Crump's Landing (confusion about the orders delayed Wallace until after dark). Guards were placed in the rear to stop stragglers at

gunpoint. Hearing that General "Bull" Nelson's division, the closest part of Buell's army, had arrived at Savannah, Grant ordered them to move to the east bank of the Tennessee opposite Pittsburg Landing. Determined Federal resistance remained on the left (Stuart) and also in a densely wooded area on the left center, dubbed by the Confederate attackers "The Hornet's Nest." Grant asked Prentiss to hold the Hornet's Nest, the key to the middle of his line, at all costs.

At half past two in the afternoon came a crushing blow both to Southern fortunes in the battle and to hopes for the Confederate cause itself. General Johnston had ridden over to the right of his lines to deal with what was intended as his main thrust, on the Federal left. He found his men still bogged down in the face of galling Union fire. Johnston ordered a charge and personally led his men in pushing the Federals back some three-quarters of a mile. While dressing their lines in the new position, the Confederates found themselves subject to enfilade fire from the left. Johnston had just ordered one regiment to wheel and meet this fire when he was struck by a stray shot and sagged on his horse. I G Harris, the Governor of Tennessee, righted the general and led his horse behind the lines. Johnston had previously dispatched his chief surgeon to the rear, to deal with Federal wounded. This act of charity probably cost him his life. The shot had cut an

artery, but the wound could easily have been treated had the surgeon been available. Without help, Johnston bled to death in a few minutes. The South thereby lost one of its greatest generals and the Confederate attack began to lose momentum. Beauregard, who had strenuously opposed the offensive tactic and was also quite ill at the time, was now in command of the Southern forces.

But the Confederate advance by no means came to an immediate halt. The Federal left was at length pushed back almost to Pittsburg Landing, threatening the arrival of Buell's reinforcements as Johnston had intended. On the Union left center, the Hornet's Nest held on with divisions commanded by Hurlbut and W H L Wallace, along with the remnants of Prentiss's division.

In all, the Rebels mounted 11 unsuccessful charges on the Hornet's Nest. But at length the Federal defenders grew exhausted, and the retreat of their own forces around them slowly exposed their flanks. Finally, Confederate General Ruggles massed 62 cannon on the position and encircled it. Federal General W H L Wallace was killed leading his division to safety out of the area. At half past five in the afternoon General Prentiss and 2200 men surrendered after some eight hours of fighting.

But the Federal's stand in the Hornet's Nest had been more

than empty heroics. The number of men and the time it took to take the position had slowed the whole Confederate thrust. It took yet more valuable time to disarm the Federal prisoners, gather them and send them to the rear, where other Southern soldiers, thinking the bulk of the Federal Army had been taken, left their positions to go peer curiously at the "captured Yanks."

It was therefore some time before Confederate forces were gathered again for what was intended to be the decisive move on the Union Army. At Pittsburg Landing the Federals had fallen back as far as the ground permitted; one more strong Rebel push would send them into the river. At that most critical moment, artillery came to the rescue of the North. Grant's artillery chief, Colonel J D Webster, opened up from a battery on high ground near the landing; the Union iron-clad gunboats *Lexington* and *Tyler*, just arrived from Savannah, opened up with long-range 64-pounders on the Rebel positions. In the face of this bombardment, the enemy advance ground to a halt. Soon came yet another moment to cheer the Federals: troops of Nelson's division of Buell's army, the desperately awaited reinforcements, were seen gathering on the east shore. In short order they were being ferried across the Tennessee.

At about six that evening, just before a final Rebel attack was to be made on Pittsburg Landing, Beauregard suspended operations to the dismay of several of his commanders. He did so partly because night was coming, partly because he was ignorant of Buell's impending arrival. His intelligence reported that Buell could not be expected to arrive in time to aid Grant, and therefore the Southerners could take time to rest and regroup.

The Confederates that night assumed they had won. Back in the captured Union camps, the Rebels celebrated with the enemy's provisions and liquor, enjoying the shelter of the tents when a storm blew in; Union troops had to bivouac outside in the torrential rain. True, the Rebels were harried by the Union gunboats, which continued to shell their positions all night, but neither that nor the rain could dampen the Southerners' sense of impending victory.

During that wet and miserable night Grant hobbled about, kept awake by the pain of his riding injury and sickened by the suffering of his wounded men. Nonetheless, he thought coolly and clearly. He saw that the next day's victory would go to whoever attacked first, and made his plans accordingly. All night, while the Confederates were celebrating, Buell's men were being transported across the Tennessee – divisions led by Crittenden, McCook and Nelson, totaling 25,000 men, all of them fresh. Lew Wallace's division of 5000 finally arrived after dark. This was entirely unknown to Beauregard, who expected the imminent arrival of 20,000 reinforcements under General Van Dorn, moving up from Arkansas.

On 7 April, at 7:30 AM, Grant's supposedly beaten Federals unleashed a well-co-ordinated counterattack on both enemy flanks, led by Lew Wallace on the Union right and Nelson, of Buell's army, on the left. Wallace began with his artillery, dueling with the enemy cannon, and sent his soldiers across a ravine on to the Southern flank; the enemy hastily withdrew with their own guns. Nelson pressed forward with equal success on the left. By 10:30 the fighting was general all along the line, and the Federals had regained much of the ground lost the previous day.

A Southern offensive developed around a peach orchard on the Union right; the Federals, having outrun their artillery, gave way for a time. At length Union artillery was moved up, and General Buell directed the assault; after a seesaw contest the Rebel lines were again driven away. By early afternoon the Confederate right had been pushed back and the Federals had reoccupied their original camps, recapturing weapons and materiel they had abandoned the day before. Beauregard mounted a strong resistance in front of the crossroads by Shiloh Church, now his headquarters; the roads there were Van Dorn's best route to reinforce Beauregard, and also the best route on which to retreat, if it came to that. Beauregard had only 20,000 men left fighting. Without Van Dorn, he saw that it would indeed come to retreat. He held on to the crossroads grimly for a time; the insignificant meetinghouse became the focal point of the battle that would bear its name.

By 2:30 that afternoon Beauregard had learned that Van Dorn had been halted by the swollen Mississippi. The Federals were pushing back his forces all along the line, casualties were mounting and straggling was becoming uncontrollable – troops fell out by the hundreds and streamed to the rear. There was only one option left: Beauregard issued orders to retreat. The Confederates withdrew toward Corinth in good order, the retreat covered by infantry and artillery under General Nathan Bedford Forrest. At three o'clock Grant personally directed a last Union charge along the road to Corinth. By five o'clock, the Rebels had retired from the field. The exhausted Federals sank into their recaptured camps and did not pursue.

In the ensuing days both sides claimed victory, and in fact, Union casualties were greater. But it was unquestionably a Union victory, if an incomplete one. The South had begun with a tactical surprise – much disputed by Grant in his memoirs, but a suprise all the same – and had fought gallantly and with great initial effect. But the Rebel attack had been poorly co-ordinated and overextended; those facts, combined with the disaster of Johnston's death, had allowed the Federals to regroup and finally to take the initiative. As is usually the case, the side that in the end held the initiative gained the victory.

Shiloh was the first battle in the Western Hemisphere to involve over 100,000 men. Casualties were appalling on both sides: of 62,682 Union effectives (by the second day), 1754 were killed, 8408 wounded and 2885 missing, for a total of 13,047 casualties; of the South's 40,335 effectives, 1723 were killed, 8012 wounded, 959 missing, for a total of 10,694.

Beauregard's defeat was to damage his prestige for some time during the war. As for Grant, he had been surprised, and the brilliance of his holding on and striking back did not erase that fact. But Lincoln, seeing things clearly from distant Washington, was soon to reply to demands for Grant's dismissal with eloquent simplicity: "I can't spare this man. He fights."

Left: *The Union resistance at the Hornet's Nest withstood eleven Rebel charges, slowing the Confederate thrust.*

Opposite top: *Wisconsin volunteers charge a New Orleans battery at Shiloh.*

Opposite bottom: *P G T Beauregard (right) succeeded Confederate General A S Johnston but was no match for Grant. Nathan Bedford Forrest (left) directed troops covering Beauregard's retreat toward Corinth.*

VICKSBURG

Alittle more than three weeks after the Battle of Shiloh ended, the commander for the Confederate Army in Virginia, Joseph E Johnston, was replaced by a man who would soon be recognized the world over as one of history's greatest generals. If Union fortunes in the Eastern Military Theater had been low before the advent of Robert E Lee, they were about to sink to their nadir. Within two months of his accession to the command of the newly named Army of Northern Virginia, Lee had utterly defeated Union General George B McClellan's massive, clumsy offensive against Richmond via the Virginia Peninsula, and a month later Lee routed McClellan's Army of the Potomac at the Second Battle of Bull Run (Second Manassas). In mid-September the two armies clashed again in the bloody, inconclusive Battle of Antietam. Some in the North professed to believe that Antietam was a Northern victory (presumably on the grounds that Lee had not actually won it), but whatever comfort Northerners drew from such fancies evaporated when Lee again smashed the advancing Army of the Potomac (now under McClellan's successor, Ambrose Burnside) at the dismal Battle of Fredericksburg in mid-December.

The high-water mark of Lee's remarkable string of victories occurred when serious campaigning resumed in the spring of 1863. Late in April, General Joseph Hooker, the hapless Burnside's successor, attempted to pin Lee's army at Fredericksburg between a combined frontal assault and right-wing envelopment. Lee repelled the frontal assault as easily as he had Burnside's, while at the same time moving the bulk of his forces so adroitly that in short order he had not only stymied the envelopment but placed it on the defensive at Chancellorsville, about ten miles west of Fredericksburg.

Opposite top: *Ambrose E Burnside commanded the Union Army of the Potomac at Fredericksburg.*

Opposite bottom: *Lincoln visits McClellan (facing him) in October 1862.*

Above: *Mississippi riverboats at Vicksburg, the principal supply center for the Southern war effort and the focus of an eight-month-long campaign by General Grant to split the entire Confederacy.*

Lee then mounted an attack on Hooker's right flank at Chancellorsville, an attack that proved so successful that by 5 May the whole 90,000-man Army of the Potomac was again in full retreat. Only the death of Lee's great lieutenant, Stonewall Jackson, marred this otherwise brilliant victory. Hardly pausing for breath, Lee next hurled the Army of Northern Virginia northwest in an invasion of Pennsylvania, a bold stroke that would shortly culminate in the most famous battle in American history.

But while Robert E Lee was dominating the Eastern Theater of the war with his tactical genius, a different kind of military genius was demonstrating his brilliance in long-range strategic planning in the Western Theater. The man was Ulysses S Grant. The complex and historic Vicksburg

Campaign of 1862-63 would be remembered as Grant's masterpiece, as Chancellorsville was Lee's.

The town of Vicksburg, Mississippi, lies atop high bluffs on the banks of the Mississippi River. It occupies the first high land on the eastern bank of the river below Memphis, some 400 miles to the north. Throughout the winter of 1862-63 the Mississippi was swollen by heavy rains, and Vicksburg overlooked hundreds of miles of flooded and swampy land and river bottom. The town was approachable by land only from the east, from Confederate territory. And the water route was impassable to most Union shipping: the bluffs before Vicksburg were bristling with fortifications and batteries that dominated the river below.

Strategically, Vicksburg was one of the two most vital towns of the Confederacy, the other being the rail center of Chattanooga. To the east through Vicksburg came food, supplies and cotton necessary to the Southern war effort. Could the North conquer the city, those supplies would be cut off and Union armies and supplies could pass unmolested through the very center of the Confederacy. It was essential to the North's grand strategy to accomplish that task.

On 25 October 1862 Ulysses S Grant was given command of the Federal Department of the Tennessee. A week after his

Left: *Union troops confront
Lee's soldiers at Burnside
Bridge in the Battle of
Antietam. The battle put the
South on the defensive and
set the scene for the failed
Union assault on
Fredericksburg.*

Below: *In the Western
Theater of the war, General
Grant mounted his Vicksburg
Campaign in the winter of
1862. By mid-May 1863 he
had begun his siege of
Vicksburg.*

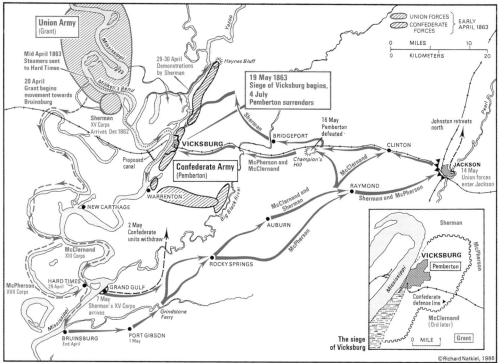

Union Army
(Grant)

Mid April 1863
Steamers sent
to Hard Times

20 April
Grant begins
movement towards
Bruinsburg

Sherman
XV Corps
Arrives Dec 1862

29-30 April
Demonstrations
by Sherman

Haynes Bluff

19 May 1863
Siege of Vicksburg begins,
4 July
Pemberton surrenders

UNION FORCES
CONFEDERATE
FORCES

EARLY
APRIL 1863

MILES   10
KILOMETERS   20

Sherman

BRIDGEPORT

16 May
Pemberton
defeated

Johnston retreats
north

CLINTON

JACKSON
14 May
Union forces
enter Jackson

Proposed
canal

VICKSBURG

Confederate Army
(Pemberton)

McPherson and
McClernand

Champion's
Hill

McClernand

WARRENTON

Big Black River

RAYMOND

McClernand and
Sherman

Sherman and McPherson

NEW CARTHAGE

2 May
Confederate
units withdraw

AUBURN

McPherson

McClernand
XIII Corps

ROCKY SPRINGS

McPherson
XVII Corps

HARD TIMES
29 April

GRAND GULF

7 May
Sherman's XV Corps
arrives

Grindstone
Ferry

The siege
of Vicksburg

Sherman

VICKSBURG

McPherson

Pemberton

Mississippi

Confederate
defense line

McClernand
(Ord later)

Grant

MILE 1

BRUINSBURG
End April

PORT GIBSON
1 May

©Richard Natkiel, 1986

Right: *For many months the Union tried to dig a canal across a bend of the Mississippi River opposite Vicksburg to allow Federal gunboats to avoid the defending Rebel batteries. The attempt was thwarted by rising waters.*

Below: *General John Pemberton, the Confederate commander in Mississippi, was forced by Grant's siege to formally surrender Vicksburg on 4 July 1863. It is considered by many to be the turning point of the war.*

appointment he began to move overland on Vicksburg. Much of the Mississippi already lay in Union hands – Admiral Farragut had conquered New Orleans in the spring of 1862 and had cleared the river up to Baton Rouge, Louisiana. Soon after, a Federal flotilla had all but destroyed a Confederate fleet on the Mississippi at Memphis and taken that city.

In November Grant moved his 40,000 men out of Jackson, Tennessee, marching south on the east side of the Mississippi toward Vicksburg. This campaign soon came to grief: on 20 December a Confederate cavalry force under General Earl van Dorn swept into the Federal base at Holly Springs, Mississippi, just south of the Tennessee border, and destroyed most of Grant's supplies. At the same time, cavalry under Nathan Bedford Forrest raided Union communication lines in western Tennessee, destroying 60 miles of railroad. The Union advance ground to a halt just as further misfortunes developed to the south.

William T Sherman, Grant's closest subordinate, had been dispatched down the Yazoo River to take possession of the landings at Vicksburg, in support of Grant's campaign. But just north of the city at Chickasaw Bluffs, Sherman's forces were severely repulsed on 27-29 December; in that action the Union suffered 1776 casualties to the South's 207. It became clear to Federal leaders that Vicksburg was going to be a tough nut indeed to crack.

Thus at the beginning of 1863 the North's war effort was stalled all over the map: Grant was apparently going nowhere, and neither were Hooker in the East or Rosecrans in Tennessee. Grant proceeded to size up his situation. An over-

Above: *Admiral David Dixon Porter commanded the Union Mississippi Squadron in the Vicksburg Campaign.*

Right: *Admiral Porter's fleet of transports, escorted by six gunboats (including his flagship* Benton), *run the Rebel blockade at Vicksburg on 16 April 1863.*

Opposite: *Confederate General Joseph E Johnston's defense of Vicksburg was thwarted both by Grant and by the enmity of Jefferson Davis, who countermanded his orders.*

land advance on Vicksburg had just been proven impossible, and the high waters made all land operations difficult, but public and political pressure from the North obliged him to do *something* – or else. Accordingly, Grant shifted his base to Young's Point, nearly opposite Vicksburg on the western (Louisiana) bank of the river, and in the first months of 1863 indulged in a series of experiments that he privately doubted would work.

The first experiment was to cut a canal across Young's Point, in hopes of moving Union boats through it and down the Mississippi. But the canal when finished could not be filled to a depth sufficient to float the ships. While the canal was in progress Grant dispatched General James B McPherson's XVII Corps to try to open a passage from Lake Providence south through the soggy landscape in order to come out on the Red River south of Vicksburg, whence steamers could move back upstream. This scheme was abandoned in March for a more promising one in the Yazoo Pass, 325 miles north of Vicksburg. There the Federals cut through a levee and the fleet steamed into the Tallahatchie River, moving south toward the Yazoo and Vicksburg. This expedition ran afoul of a hastily constructed Rebel work named Fort Pemberton in honor of Vicksburg's commander, General John C

Pemberton. For six days in mid-March the little fort turned back the best efforts of the Federal fleet to pass. Grant then moved on to his fourth and final experiment, an attempt to push Federal ships north through a tangled mass of streams and backwaters called Steel's Bayou. Trying to move up through the tiny waterways to the Yazoo, Admiral David D Porter's boats were obstructed by trees, some of them felled by the Confederates, who then attacked the Union boats on 19 March. Porter had to be rescued by Sherman's corps. There ended Grant's experiments, all of them fantastically difficult and round-about ways to traverse the few miles that separated Vicksburg from the Union base, which was now at Millikin's Bend just across the river from Vicksburg.

Grant had tried every possible water route to Vicksburg: now he had to go overland, and do it soon. The whole progress of the war in the West was on his shoulders, and the West was where the Confederacy must ultimately be beaten – in its own territory. So Grant devised a new plan. The high water had receded enough so that he could march his men south on the Louisiana side of the river. Once south of Vicksburg, they had somehow to cross the Mississipi, which could be done only by running the Federal fleet directly past the fearsome Vicksburg batteries; the ships would meet the army

McClernand's considerable chagrin. On 29 March Grant sent McClernand's XIII Corps to forge a trail from Millikin's Bend south to New Carthage. The men set about tearing down plantation homes, and anything else handy, to build bridges across the tangled waterways on the Louisiana side. Admiral Porter stood by to provide troop transport and supplies.

By 16 April it was time for the first critical gamble of the campaign – running Union ships past Vicksburg. The ships, six gunboats and several transports of Admiral Porter's fleet, were manned by a few volunteers; in the holds waited men with boards, cotton and gunny sacks to patch up holes made by enemy fire. The vulnerable transport ships were padded with cotton bales and had barges of coal and forage lashed alongside. Around 11:00 PM the ships began floating silently downstream. An hour later they were opposite Vicksburg, where they were spotted by the Confederate defenders. The Rebel batteries opened up, turning the bluffs into a sheet of flame, and the ships put on steam.

Remarkably, Porter succeeded in running the batteries, losing only one ship and a few barges, and the battered flotilla came to rest at Hard Times, where Grant's army was gathering. On 22 April more transports and barges ran the gauntlet. Meanwhile, Sherman made a feint at Haines's Bluff, moving his corps up and down the river and the shore until Pemberton, in Vicksburg, was convinced a major attack was coming there. Once the Confederates were properly distracted, Sherman marched to join Grant below Vicksburg.

Much as Pemberton was confused by the feint at Haines's Bluff, however, he was more concerned by the other Federal diversion designed to screen Grant's crossing of the Mississippi. General Benjamin H Grierson and 1700 cavalrymen left LaGrange, Tennessee, on 17 April, riding south through Mississippi. A worried Pemberton sent cavalry in pursuit (at the same time marching men to meet Sherman's imaginary offensive at Haines's Bluff). After two weeks of hard riding, evading pursuers, raiding and skirmishing, Grierson arrived at Federally-held Baton Rouge on 2 May. His men had ridden 600 miles in 16 days, accounted for 100 Rebel casualties,

downriver and ferry the troops across. (Admiral Farragut had moved ships past the batteries in the summer of 1862, so perhaps it was possible.) If this could be done, Grant would then move his men northwest across Mississippi, cut communications between Vicksburg and the Confederacy and lay siege to the city. Meanwhile, to screen the operation, Sherman and Colonel R H Grierson would pursue diversionary operations, Sherman on Haines's Bluff near Vicksburg and Grierson moving his cavalry south from Tennessee through Mississippi. Thus Grant planned four carefully co-ordinated operations – his army, Porter's fleet, Sherman's corps and Grierson's cavalry – involving many thousands of men and horses, a fleet of ships and thousands of square miles of land. To take Vicksburg, many things had to work perfectly in concert, and Washington had to co-operate as well.

This latter element of Grant's requirements was as undependable as any. He had already run afoul of a secret river expedition on Vicksburg planned in Washington by a politically appointed Volunteer general, John A McClernand: this expedition was in effect competing with Grant's for the same prize. Having kept Grant in the dark for some time about McClernand, General-in-Chief Halleck finally scotched that expedition and put McClernand's forces under Grant – to

Right: *Shirley House,
headquarters of General
Grant during the siege of
Vicksburg.*

Below: *General John A
McClernand had been put in
charge of a secretly planned
expedition to Vicksburg
before coming under Grant's
command.*

taken 500 prisoners, destroyed 50 miles of railroad and much enemy weaponry, captured 1000 horses and mules – and suffered only 24 casualties. It was to be remembered as one of the most brilliant cavalry exploits of the war.

Grant, meanwhile, had run into resistance trying to cross his troops at Grand Gulf, where on 29 April 17 gunboats failed to reduce a Confederate garrison. Moving a little farther south, Grant crossed his army unopposed at Bruinsburg the next day. The Confederates then pulled out of Grand Gulf and met Grant's overland advance at Port Gibson on 1 May. In a day of fighting amid hills and deep ravines, Grant flanked the 8000 Confederates and brushed them out of the way before their reinforcements could arrive. The Northern forces – the corps of Sherman (XV), McPherson (XVII) and McClernand (XIII) – then pushed northeast across Mississippi, skirmishing constantly with Rebel forces in the rear.

Grant was planning so far to march south and join General Nathaniel P Banks (another politically appointed general of volunteers, who at the outbreak of the war was Governor of Massachusetts) in moving on Confederate-held Port Hudson, on the Mississippi to the south. Learning that Banks was busy with what was to become the extensive – and ill-fated – Red River Campaign, Grant made a bold change in plans that was destined to elevate him to the ranks of the great generals in history. Against the advice of his staff, he decided to cut away from his supply and communications lines and move into the rear of Vicksburg, first taking Jackson, the capital of the state, in the east. Then, having taken care of any potential enemy reinforcements to Vicksburg, he would besiege the city. In military terms, he would *defeat the enemy in detail* before they had the chance to concentrate superior forces against him. His army would march with all the supplies it could carry and would forage in the countryside; now Southern civilians would have to bear directly the cost of war.

Grant's opponent in Jackson was one of the best generals in the Confederacy – Joseph E Johnston. He had only somewhat recovered from wounds he had received during the Peninsular Campaign and was desperately trying to accumulate enough forces to oppose Grant. Arriving in Jackson the evening of the 13th, Johnston was so ill that he did much of his work in bed.

As Grant moved toward Jackson he sent a detachment to feint toward Vicksburg, where Pemberton was still trying to figure out what the Federals were up to. Sherman crossed his corps at Grand Gulf on 6 May, and by the 12th Grant was approaching Jackson with 44,000 men. That day McPherson's corps routed a Rebel detachment at Raymond, Mississippi; leaving McClernand in that town to protect his rear, Grant arrived before Jackson on the 13th. That night Johnston wrote to Pemberton in Vicksburg, ordering him to move on Grant's rear.

Johnston had only 6000 men to oppose the Federals' two corps; Confederate reinforcements were on the way, but Grant had no intention of waiting for their arrival, or for Pemberton to move. On 14 May, McPherson and Sherman easily stormed Jackson: that night Grant slept in the room Johnston had occupied the night before. Johnston moved his troops north, writing the recalcitrant Pemberton to cut Grant's supply line and then join forces.

But Pemberton had two problems with this order: one, Grant in fact had no supply line, and two, Confederate President Davis had ordered Pemberton to stay in Vicksburg. Thus Pemberton, already perplexed, was caught between contradictory orders from his government and from his superior, Johnston. He managed to satisfy neither very well.

Having first spent a fruitless 15 May looking for the non-existent Union supply line to the south, Pemberton turned his troops around and went east to join Johnston. The Confederate troops were exhausted, having marched in every direction for days without finding the enemy. Grant had already foreseen the Confederate move and had gone with McClernand and McPherson to meet Pemberton. (Sherman was left in Jackson to destroy manufacturing centers and railroads, a task which, as always, he performed with a vengeance.) At Champion's Hill, a small knoll in the countryside between Vicksburg and Jackson, the forces of Grant and Pemberton collided on 16 May.

Champion's Hill saw the hardest day's fighting of the campaign. The forces engaged were not radically unequal: Grant had 29,000 men of McPherson's and McLernand's corps, and Pemberton had some 22,000. (Sherman, ordered out of Jackson in the morning, arrived after the battle.) McClernand made contact with the Rebel left flank about 9:30 AM; however, he waited over four hours to make what should have been the initial attack. This gave Pemberton time to shift troops to meet McPherson's assault on his right flank at about eleven. Had McClernand attacked promptly in the morning, the Federals could probably have overwhelmed Pemberton's army and marched unopposed into Vicksburg. The fighting surged back and forth indecisively for hours, Champion's Hill changing hands repeatedly. At one point Logan's division of McPherson's corps moved on the rear of the Confederate right, cutting off Pemberton's only road of retreat; Grant, not knowing this, uncovered the road again by moving these troops to reinforce his center. Pemberton soon made use of the road, pulling his forces back just after three in the afternoon. The Confederates withdrew, bedraggled but in fair order, to the Big Black River, closely pursued by Grant's men. The casualties in the day's fighting at Champion's Hill were 2441 for the Union, 3851 for the South. Grant points out in his memoirs that Pemberton should then have evacuated Vicks-

Below: *US Signal Corps headquarters at Vicksburg. The static front made the use of telegraphy practical.*

burg and marched north to join Johnston; this in fact was
what Johnston, knowing Vicksburg was now doomed in any
case, wanted Pemberton to do. Instead, Pemberton pulled
back toward the city, leaving a rear guard before the Big
Black River. On 17 May Grant's forces attacked this position,
Sherman's corps overwhelming the enemy center. Many
Confederates were forced into the river to swim across or
drown. The remaining Southerners soon noticed that a Federal force was heading for the only bridge. Something of a
footrace ensued, the Confederates reaching the bridge first,
while their artillery remained behind, slowing the Northerners until they were captured. As the Confederates withdrew they burned the bridge and Federal pursuit came to a
halt while engineers constructed a new one.

The action at Big Black River produced one of those fortui-
tous moments that can affect profoundly the course of wars
and of nations. As Grant was observing the battle, a messenger appeared with an order from General-in-Chief Halleck. Dated several days previous, the order directed Grant to
retire without delay to Grand Gulf and then to move in support of Banks at Port Hudson. Grant and the messenger

began to debate whether or not the order was still relevant: at
that moment Grant heard a cheer denoting a successful
charge. Exclaiming "See that charge! I think it is too late to
abandon this campaign," he leaped on to his horse and rode
toward the action. The messenger was never seen again. Had
he had time to convince Grant to obey the order, Vicksburg
might never have fallen.

That night the beaten Rebels marched back into town. One
of the soldiers remembered: "By nightfall the fugitive and dis-
heveled troops were pouring into the streets of Vicksburg,
and the citizens beheld with dismay the army that had gone
out to fight for their safety returning to them in the character
of a wild, tumultuous and mutinous mob." On 18 May Johnston notified Richmond that defense of the city was hopeless.
Grant, meanwhile, sent a detachment to keep Johnston at
bay. Thus Pemberton was bottled up, and Johnston had been
rendered helpless.

While his army moved across the new bridge on 18 May,
Grant and Sherman stood surveying the defenses of Vicksburg, the goal of so many months of complex and frustrating
campaigning. Sherman observed that up to this moment he

Left: *On 25 June Federal mines were exploded under the Rebel defenses. Union soldiers who rushed through the crater were slaughtered by defenders firing down on them.*

Below: *A view of Confederate defenses behind Vicksburg.*

Overleaf: *A depiction of General Pemberton's surrender to Grant at Vicksburg.*

IMPORTANT FROM AMERICA!!
Awful Slaughter at Vicksburg,
And Elsewhere,
The Bloody Conflict between the North & South
CONTINUED!

We regret to say that this unnatural war seems still to rush upon the unhappy Yanky with fearful impetnosity, so as to stun the entire population and saturate the States of America with blood, by sacrificing the lives of hundreds of thousands of honest men, at the whim or caprice of a few noxious individuals. Federal accounts state that the siege still continues, —and, that the incredible number of 3,600 bombs were thrown into the city of Vicksburg in an hour! The streets are ploughed up with shot and shell, and that the inhabitants dwell in caves which they have excavated in the sides of the Bluff!

In the force under Banks and Sheridan there was a battalion of Negroes, who are said to have fought well. They suffered terribly, for out of a regiment of 900, 600 were killed or wounded in an hour!

The Prize Court at Key West has laid down the law of confiscation so as to insure the condemnation of every British Ship a Federal vessel may seize,—'Any vessel bound to Nassau, with the intention of sailing from thence to a blockaded port, is liable to condemnation." As the prize court constitutes itself sole judge of the intention, and as Matamoras has been, de facto blockaded, all British vessels bound for that port will, of course, be at once condemned. The Key West correspondent of the New-York Herald has good reason to say that "nowhere else is prise law rigidly enforced, vessels being con-

demned at the rate of two each week."

Although 49,688 emigrants had arrived in New York from Ireland since the first of January, 1863, and though the negroes are said to be the "best hope of restoring the Union," the enrollment is being enforced.

Queenstown, Saturday,—The following is the latest "correspondence" from Vicksburg. One regiment only, the 22nd Iowa Volunteers, commanded by Colonel William M. Stone, by almost superhuman efforts, and after immense loss, planted its colours on the rebel rampart. There it remained all day long, the rebels hourly demanding aid, until at nightfall, after having been exposed all day to a destructive fire, the lieutenant-colonel and 15 men only remained and they were taken in great triumph to Vicksburg. Every man who entered the fort in the morning was killed or wounded except those sixteen. Colonel Stone was struck in the arm whilst on the skirline, loudly calling for reinforcements. It was a stupid blunder, or crime, to storm the works at all. It needs not a military eye to discover that it is impossible to lead men over an abrupt embankment twenty feet high, with ditches from ten to twelve feet deep. It was doubtless, necessary that the experiment should be tried. It has proven a costly one. Twenty-five hundred killed and wounded is a fearful loss.

The northern are evidently constructing a new

line of works between the outer line opposed to us and the city. While the charge was being made on the 22nd some of our sharp-shooters, posted in the trees overlooking the fortifications, could plainly see contrabands and white men digging for dear life.

OUR LOSSES

I regret to learn that Colonel Abbot, of the 30th Iowa, was killed on the 22nd instant. He was a brave officer, and his loss is unusually regretted. In the battle of Champion's Hill, on the 16th, instant, the tenth Iowa lost, killed, wounded, and missing, one hundred and sixty-one men. Among the killed were three commissioned officers and 7 wounded. In the recent charge on the fortifications the twenty-second Iowa lost two hundred and fifty men: General Stevenson's Brigade, two hundred and sixty; General Ransom's Brigade, three hundred and fifty-eight. General Carr's division, five hundred; General Blair's division, five hundred and fifty; General Steele's division, heavily, estimated six hundred; General Osterhaus' division two hundred, estimated; and General Smith's three hundred and fifty, estimated. This is rather under than over the estimate.

CANNONADING.

To-day there has been vigorous cannonading at intervals from batteries on the right and left of the railroad. A misdirected shot fell in our own ranks killing three soldiers of the thirty-second Ohio, and seriously wounding as many more.

Over one hundred women and children have been killed by our bombardment.

New-York, June 14—General Banks flocially reports that the conduct of the Negro troops has been most praiseworthy, and there is no longer any doubt

that the Government will find in the Negroes effective supporters.

General Banks' loss from the 23rd to the 30th, ult., was 1,000 men, including many of his ablest officers.

General Sherman has died of his wounds.

General Neal Dow is also dangerously wounded.

ANOTHER BATTLE,

Three brigades of Federal Cavalry, and 2,000 infantry crossed the Rappahannock on Tuesday at Beverley Ford, and had a severe engagement with General Stuart's cavalry, lasting all day, when the Confederates received heavy infantry reinforcements, and the Federals recrossed the river bringing away their dead and wounded. Sharp firing was kept up from the confederate rifle pits during the crossing, and 40 of the Federals were killed or wounded. A portion of Federal land and naval forces at Yorktown, made an incursion into King William County, Virginia, via the Mattapony River. On the 4th inst. a Foundry at Ayltes, with all its machinery, several mills, and large quantities of grain, were destroyed, and many horses, mules, and cattle were captured. The expedition returned to Yorktown the following day.

The agricultural resources of the Yazoo country are described as being most abundant

---

John F. Nugent and Co., Steam-Machine Printers, 35, New-Row West, Dublin.   N.B.—No connection with any other person of the name.

Left: *European interest in the Civil War was intense. An Irish newspaper reports on the siege at Vicksburg.*

Above: *Drawing by a field artist of Grant receiving Pemberton's 3 July request for surrender negotiations.*

had been unsure of their ultimate success, and added generously that it was the end of one of the greatest campaigns in military history. Sherman was right enough, except for the fact that Vicksburg itself was not yet conquered. To be sure, it would take a miracle to save it – but the South had been known to produce miracles. The fortifications around Vicksburg had been seven months in the making. They included a line nine miles long, with nine forts as strong points. The works took advantage of the broken ground around the city, which made it an excellent place to defend and a dangerous one to attack. Restless at the idea of a protracted siege, Grant attempted an assault on 19 May, resulting only in a few yards' gain toward the city. Another assault was mounted on the afternoon of the 22nd: it proved a costly failure. The 13,000 Confederate defenders turned back 35,000 Federals and inflicted 3200 casualties; Southern casualties were around 500. (Grant was later to write that he regretted this assault, as well as a later and more disastrous one at Cold Harbor in 1864). Within Vicksburg, the spirits of Pemberton's men revived in the aftermath of their success.

Grant then settled into a siege, gradually extending his lines over fifteen miles in a bear-hug around Vicksburg. Federal supplies and reinforcements arrived steadily until the Northerners numbered some 71,000. Washington co-operated fully: as Halleck wrote to Lincoln, "To open the Mississippi River would be better than the capture of forty Richmonds."

The opposing lines were at times only a few yards apart; soldiers of the two sides regularly exchanged news and gibes. Sharpshooters picked off anyone careless enough to poke his head above the ramparts. On 25 June and 1 July Federal mines under the defenses were blown up, but the planned attacks did not develop.

Within the city the civilians dug into the hills to escape incessant shelling from Union batteries and gunboats. Citizens

and soldiers starved together: by late June most of the army's mules had been consumed. One soldier recalled that he and his companions came positively to enjoy a hearty helping of fried rat for breakfast.

A major Federal assault on the starving garrison was planned for 6 July, but on the 3rd, as Southern fortunes in the East were foundering in distant Gettysburg, white flags appeared on the ramparts of Vicksburg. Union troops danced, cheered and set off cannon. Soon Pemberton, an old army acquaintance of Grant, appeared, and Grant asked of him the same unconditional surrender he had demanded at Fort Donelson. When Pemberton curtly declined these terms, Grant hastened to negotiate. While the generals of the opposing staffs discussed terms, Grant and Pemberton sat on a hillside frostily passing the time of day. After some discussion Pemberton agreed to surrender the garrison on 4 July, Independence Day, and Grant agreed to parole the Confederates rather than imprison them. (To this point in the war, prisoners of both sides were often paroled until exchanged.)

At three o'clock in the afternoon of 4 July 1863, 30,000 ragged and hungry Confederates filed out of Vicksburg to stack their arms. Union troops watched in silence: as he would in future victories, Grant forbade any demonstration of triumph by his troops (though one unit was heard to cheer the valor of the Confederates). Federals were seen reaching into their supplies to give food to the Rebels. In the northeast at Gettysburg, the South had just lost a great battle. But here in Vicksburg the Confederacy had, in effect, already lost the war. Port Hudson, the last Confederate stronghold on the river, fell to Banks on 8 July. The South was cut in two, for the Mississippi lay open to the North. In Washington a jubilant Lincoln wrote "The Father of Waters runs unvexed to the sea."

Grant had carried off one of the greatest campaigns in history, showing a gift for wide-ranging strategic planning that took advantage of the North's superiority in materiel and manpower and that was based more on maneuver than on fighting. Grant was soon to pit his strategic brilliance against the tactical genius on the battlefield of Robert E Lee: then the war would become a duel of strategy versus tactics.

GETTYSBURG

In June of 1863 the two great armies of the East were on the march, moving inexorably toward the convulsion that everyone knew had to come some time, and which both sides fervently prayed would settle everything once and for all.

The Confederate Army of Northern Virginia had whipped the Yankees three times in the past 12 months – at the Second Bull Run, Fredericksburg and Chancellorsville, with Antietam more or less a draw – and they were led by a man they considered the greatest general in the world. If ever an army felt invincible, the Army of Northern Virginia did that summer. And now they were headed toward Washington.

But things were not so good as they seemed for the South. Lee's decision to invade the North for the second time was made partly in desperation. The situation in the Confederacy was critical: the Mississippi was all but lost; badly needed European recognition had not come; the Union blockade was tightening; anti-war sentiment in the North was fading; Southern finances were collapsing. The only hope for the Confederacy now, Lee reasoned, was a decisive victory that would win the war in one stroke. On the desk of Jefferson Davis was a letter to be given to Lincoln after that victory: a letter from the victor to the vanquished, proposing terms for peace.

But Lee's convictions were not shared by his second in command, James Longstreet, whom Lee affectionately called "my old war horse." Longstreet objected to the invasion from

Right: *General Robert E Lee in the uniform he preferred – that of a colonel of cavalry. For three days at Gettysburg he ordered repeated attacks on the Union lines.*

Opposite: *General Joseph ("Fighting Joe") Hooker, depicted leading a Union charge at Antietam, was relieved as commander of the Army of the Potomac only a few days before the onset of fighting at Gettysburg.*

the beginning, proposing instead a plan to hold Hooker and his Union Army of the Potomac with two divisions while sending the rest to Tennessee, where they would join Bragg and Johnston in fighting Rosecrans. This move would probably force Grant away from his siege of Vicksburg, paralyze the North and threaten Kentucky and Ohio.

It was a good plan and might very well have worked, but Lee rejected it. His sights, as always, were fixed above all on his beloved Virginia: he wanted to end the Union threat to his exhausted state and find food for his army in the farms of Pennsylvania. The most Longstreet could get from Lee was agreement that the campaign should be offensive in strategy

but defensive in tactics. And in the end Lee would not abide by that notion either.

Lee's first move was to reorganize his army into three corps with integral artillery: those led by Longstreet, A P Hill and the brilliant and eccentric Richard S Ewell. Added to this was an oversize cavalry division under Jeb Stuart – in all, some 89,000 men.

The Confederate Army pulled out of its old field of triumph, Fredericksburg, Virginia, on 3 June, leaving Hill behind to fool Hooker and the Army of the Potomac. But Joe Hooker was not be fooled this time. Union reconnaissance parties skirmished with the Rebels at Franklin's Crossing (5 June) and Brandy

Above: *An engraving shows Rebel cavalry crossing the Potomac into Maryland on 11 June 1863.*

Left: *Inhabitants and Union guards flee Wrightsville, Pennsylvania, as it is occupied by General Ewell's forces on 28 June.*

Station (8 June) and established that Lee was on the march. Concentrating around Culpeper, Virginia, Lee sent Ewell to clear away R H Milroy's Federals in the Shenandoah Valley, which was accomplished easily enough. It was hoped this operation would keep Hooker away from Richmond and put him in a defensive posture. It did just that. The state militias of Maryland and Pennsylvania hastened to organize against Lee, but their resistance was pathetically inadequate. So far, things were not going badly for the campaign.

By mid-June Hill had left Fredericksburg, and the whole Army of Northern Virginia was on the move through Maryland to the northwest, circling Washington. Paralleling them to the east like a shadow were Hooker and the Army of the Potomac, 122,000 strong, staying between the Rebel Army and Washington. Hooker had entreated his superiors to let

him march on Richmond, but General-in-Chief Henry Halleck insisted on maintaining a defensive posture. Meanwhile, Halleck was trying to find some way to get around Hooker's political supporters and give the army to someone else – Hooker's humiliation at Chancellorsville was not to be overlooked.

As the South's and North's main forces marched northwest, the two cavalries, both on reconnaissance, fought a running series of skirmishes. Now the Federal horsemen (under General Alfred Pleasonton) had enough confidence and experience to challenge Jeb Stuart. Though largely indecisive, these skirmishes served to keep the Rebel cavalry at a distance from the Federal infantry: as a result, Stuart was not at all sure where the bulk of the enemy was.

This problem was soon compounded when Stuart proposed to Lee that his men repeat an old ploy of theirs – riding completely around the Federal Army. Lee agreed to the plan. Stuart set out on what seemed like a good bit of fun, but soon found he was getting more than he had bargained for. The Federals were spread out far more widely than expected; to avoid them Stuart had to detour farther and farther east. He was ultimately to be out of touch with Lee for ten days and did not rejoin the army until the second night of the battle. The effect on Lee's campaign was devastating – the Confederate Army was in effect marching blindfolded into extremely dangerous enemy territory.

Thus Lee moved into Pennsylvania, his forces widely separated, not knowing that Hooker had crossed the Potomac (15-16 June), and that the Federal Army was squarely on the Confederate flank and the shortest road to Richmond. Finally, on 28 June, a spy revealed to Lee that the Federals were concentrating around Frederick, Maryland. Moreover, the Army of the Potomac had a new commander. In late June, Hooker had ordered the XII Corps to join the Federal garrison at Harpers Ferry and operate on the rear of Lee's army. Halleck countermanded the order and, as was hoped, this blow to his authority was too much for Hooker. He resigned on 28 June and was replaced by General George G Meade, who, despite his protests, was chosen over his superior John Reynolds and ordered to command virtually on the eve of battle.

It was the fifth change of command in ten months for the Army of the Potomac, and a good sign of how desperate the authorities in Washington were. By now the soldiers scarcely cared any more: they had long since lost enthusiasm for the whole race of generals, and most of them knew little of Meade. He was a drawn and gloomy man, still suffering from the effects of a wound at White Oak Swamp, and his foul temper was legendary among his subordinates. The terrible burden of responsibility that dropped on him so unexpectedly served only to make Meade still more gloomy and irascible.

Above: *General George G Meade replaced Hooker on 28 June 1863.*

Below: *Alarmed by Lee's advance, Baltimore prepared its defenses.*

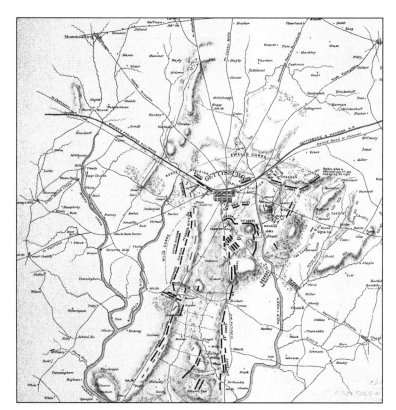

Left: *Map of the battlefield at Gettysburg showing the troop positions on 2 July.*

But if not truly brilliant, Meade was still a tough and competent general. Hearing the news, Lee prophesied accurately "General Meade will make no blunder on my front." Meade's army consisted by now of seasoned, hardened soldiers. Cynical as they had become about commanders, they were ready to do as they were told. They had seen victory elude their grasp time and time again and knew it was not their fault; they were ready to win if only they could find a leader who would let them.

Realizing the enemy was on his flank, Lee decided to concentrate at the nearest place handy, which happened to be Gettysburg, Pennsylvania, a little town with a great many road crossings. Lee was by no means planning a battle there: he could not in any case, for with Stuart gone he was still unsure just where the Army of the Potomac was. He was concentrating simply in order to discourage operations on the rear of his army. If it came to battle, his intended position was to be nearby Cashtown, which would be ideal for defense.

Meade, however, had made the same decision – to concentrate at Gettysburg – and for the same reason: convenience. Like Lee, he was not entirely certain where his enemy was. His real goal was to settle into a defensive position at Pipe Creek, 15 miles southeast of Gettysburg. Thus the most terrible battle ever fought on American soil was about to break out by accident. The course of the battle would also be significantly determined by happenstance – the Confederate Army was by then fairly tightly concentrated, the Union Army spread out. Jeb Stuart was still skylarking, Lee was still blindfolded and A P Hill's men had heard they might find some shoes in town.

On 1 July John Buford's Federal cavalry division was scouting in Gettysburg. Buford, a tough old cavalry soldier, had felt a premonition they would run into trouble. Watching from a ridge just west of town that morning, Buford saw the trouble coming: a column of enemy troops, preceded by skirmishers, slogging toward town. They were Harry Heth's division of Hill's corps, and they were looking for shoes not Yankees.

The 2500 Federal cavalry dismounted, formed a thin line of battle from McPherson's Ridge north to Seminary Ridge and began firing away with their new Spencer repeating carbines. The Rebels spread out and returned fire. By ten in the morning the fighting was hot, and Confederates seemed to be pouring in from everywhere. General William D Pender had arrived to support Heth, and the Federal cavalrymen were now badly outnumbered, but still they held on. Buford had sent a plea for help to John Reynolds and the I Corps. About ten o'clock in the morning Reynolds arrived just in front of his corps, expertly surveyed the situation and rushed to position his arriving infantry. They included John Gibbon's old bunch, the black-hatted Iron Brigade, a legendary outfit since their first battle at the Second Bull Run. (They were now under Solomon J Merideth.) As they fell into line the men of the Iron Brigade could hear the Rebels observing "Here are those damned black-hat fellers agin. . . .'Tain't no militia - that's the Army of the Potomac!"

Hill's Confederates were now falling into line in waves. The I Corps took over from the exhausted cavalrymen and began to stabilize the Union position a little. The Federals were slowly pushed back from McPherson's Ridge to Seminary Ridge, but they were not in retreat. Hundreds of Southerners were captured after vicious fighting in a railroad cut to the South. General Reynolds rode behind his lines, strengthening the position. He was considered by many the best soldier in the Union Army, the man who should have been commander of the Army of the Potomac all along. But a sharpshooter's bullet knocked Reynolds dead from his saddle early in the action. Without a commander now, his men held the line.

At noon there was an ominous lull. Heth formed his Confederates south of the Cashtown road. Federal Generals Abner Doubleday and James Wadsworth dressed their lines along and in front of Seminary Ridge as the rest of the I Corps arrived and fell into line. About 1:00 PM Oliver O Howard's XI Corps, called forward urgently, began arriving; the divisions of Carl Shurz and Francis Barlow took position to the north, on the Federal right. Howard decided to leave an artillery reserve on Cemetery Hill, just south of town. His placement of the battery on Cemetery Hill turned out to be one of those small decisions that win battles.

Lee by early afternoon had decided to throw everything he had at the Federals. Ewell, leading Jackson's old corps, descended from the north on to the Federal right. The luckless XI Corps were flanked and finally caved in, with Barlow critically wounded. Frantic calls went back to the nearest Union corps,

Daniel E Sickles's (III) and Henry W Slocum's (XII). The XI Corps fled through Gettysburg and there, in the streets, ran into large masses of Rebels.

The collapse of the XI Corps in the north made the position of Doubleday, now commanding the I Corps to the south, untenable. Finally, I Corps was pulled back.

On the left of the Union line the Iron Brigade had been ordered to hold out to the last extremity. This they did as Rebels swarmed on to them from three sides. Time and again they requested General Wadsworth to let them retreat; time and again Wadsworth refused. One stand of colors had five color-bearers shot from under the same flag, the last being the commanding general. Finally, the devastated Iron Brigade pulled back to barricades at the Seminary and made another stand before Hill pushed them back again.

The Confederates pressed on relentlessly, scattering the I Corps before them. It was an all-too-familiar story for the Army of the Potomac: Lee had massed his troops to gain local superiority and was crushing his enemy piece by piece. But there remained Howard's Union artillery reserve to the south on Cemetery Hill. As evening descended, General Winfield Scott Hancock arrived at that position. He had been sent by Meade to take charge and to survey the situation.

Right: *General John J Reynolds, considered one of the Union's best commanders, was killed in the first day's fighting.*

At first sight it was very bad. From the hill Hancock saw the Federals in confused rout. The I Corps had only 2400 men left of its original 10,000. The Iron Brigade was virtually ruined; its 24th Michigan Regiment had lost 399 of 496 men. The XI Corps had 4000 captured in the wild melee as they fled through Gettysburg. There were at most only 5000 men left available out of two corps.

Shouting and cursing, Hancock slowly rallied the stragglers around Howard's battery on Cemetery Hill. As dark came on he had a serviceable position; somehow the I and XI Corps were in line of battle again. Hancock saw that this hill was not a bad place to be, in fact might be a very good position indeed. Noticing that Culp's Hill, just to the west, might be vulnerable, Hancock sent some of the I Corps survivors over to occupy it. Another serviceable position, maybe.

Across the way, Ewell was taking a good look at Cemetery Hill. Lee had asked him to assault it "if possible." That courteous proviso would have inspired Stonewall Jackson to move mountains. But Ewell was no Jackson, and he was plagued with an odd paralysis of will in these days. He decided not to try to take Cemetery Hill. Had he tried, American history might have been different. That position, so vulnerable that night, was to become the foundation of the Union line.

Nonetheless, the South had clearly won the day on the first

of July. It had pushed the enemy back and inflicted a terrible toll on the Union Army. A confident Lee made plans for an all-out attack as early as possible next morning; his men would walk right over the enemy, just as they had so many times before. Yet things were, again, less good than they seemed for the South. Lee had been drawn into battle at a time and on ground not of his own choosing. With Stuart still away, Lee did not know exactly where Meade's forces were. Jackson was gone, and Longstreet recalcitrant. The enemy was in its own territory, fighting for its own soil. And though the Union Army had been forced back, it had been driven on to positons that were stronger than anyone, North or South, seemed to realize that night – except perhaps for Hancock, who surveyed the area with increasing satisfaction.

This time there were to be no uncommitted corps in the Union Army, as there had been at Antietam and Chancellorsville. Meade was cautious, too much so in the long run, but this time he was going to give it everything he had. All night and next morning he moved troops into position on high ground, the lines spreading out from Cemetery Hill. He was most worried about his right flank to the north, which Ewell had smashed before. To protect this flank the Unions lines bent around the hills to the north, Slocum's XII Corps from Culp's Hill south, Howard and the XI Corps bending from the side of Culp's Hill to Cemetery Hill. Below that, the I Corps

Opening engagement.

Returning with prolonge.

Shelled out.

Position on the 3rd and 4th July.

Leaving the field, July 5th.

Above: *Drawings of experiences of the 9th Massachusetts battery at Gettysburg.*

Right: *General George Meade's headquarters on Cemetery Ridge. The photograph is by Alexander Gardner, one of Mathew Brady's associates.*

Opposite: *A Union encampment at Gettysburg.*

(now under General John Newton since Reynolds's death) and Hancock's II Corps stretched south along Cemetery Ridge; Daniel E Sickles's III Corps was on the left flank, from the end of Cemetery Ridge to the Round Tops. George G Sykes's V Corps was to the rear in reserve; John Sedgwick's Corps was still moving up. Meade established his headquarters in a shabby farmhouse on the Taneytown Road, behind the center of his line.

Good as his ground was, however, Meade's concern for the right flank – he feared the enemy could get around it to his rear – led him to build up the right and stint the left flank, especially the Round Tops, which thus became his weak points. It was just that left flank that Lee was planning to strike on the second day of battle. Once again, Longstreet had demurred – it seemed to him impossible to assault the enemy on those heights. Instead he proposed a strategic envelopment on the right, moving around behind the Federals and coming between them and Washington; then the Union Army would have to come down from those hills and fight it out where the Confederates wanted them.

Lee would have none of this: he would strike the Union left, around the Round Tops. If he could overrun these positions he would roll up the Federal line like a rug. The Confederate Army was then stretched around the fishhook shape of Meade's lines: Ewell on the left with the divisions of Johnson, Early and Rodes; Hill in the center with Pender and Anderson's divisions (Heth's in reserve); Longstreet on the left, leading the attack with Hood and McLaws. The attack was to sweep obliquely from left to right; Ewell was instructed to begin a strong diversion on the right when he heard Longstreet's guns.

A workable enough plan, but on 2 July it was bungled by everybody – though there was enough of a blunder on the

Union side to give Lee's plan a good chance of working. To begin with, Ewell balked at attacking entrenched Union positions on Culp's and Cemetery hills; he made only a few ineffectual efforts during the day, far less than the major diversion intended. In any case, Ewell never got his signal from the right during the morning. Longstreet, supposed to attack on the Confederate right at dawn, delayed through the morning and into the afternoon, saying he was waiting for Pickett's fresh division, which had not yet arrived. Jackson was sorely missed indeed.

Longstreet's delay nearly gave the Federals enough rope to hang themselves. The blunder was accomplished by Union General Daniel E Sickles, who felt the ground occupied by his III Corps on the left flank, along the southern part of Cemetery Ridge, was not high enough; besides, there were Rebels out there moving toward his left. Itching for a fight, Sickles moved the III Corps forward without orders to slightly higher ground on a line from the Peach Orchard through the Wheat Field to Devil's Den. Watching from the heights, Generals Hancock and Gibbon saw Sickles's salient forming and accurately prophesied the outcome. About four o'clock in the afternoon a furious Meade rode over and ordered Sickles to pull the line back. As they argued, an earsplitting cannonade erupted square on Sickles's left flank – 46 of Longstreet's guns. Meade curtly observed that it was too late to pull back now: the III Corps would have to fight it out as best they could.

While part of the II Corps was ordered by Meade into Sickles's original position on Cemetery Ridge, Confederate infantry under John B Hood and Lafayette McLaws struck Sickles's salient at about five o'clock. The rest of the Union Army looked on helplessly as Hood's men, despite the wounding of Hood himself, routed the Union position in Devil's Den and swarmed around the left flank and up Round Top. By six, Sickles had been carried from the field minus a leg and General David B Birney had taken command, his left already giving way.

As Meade desperately shifted troops from his center and

Left: *Lee's headquarters (Mrs. Thompson's house) on the Chambersburg Pike.*

Below: *Southerners attempt to break the Union defensive line at Cemetery Hill.*

Above: *Fighting at the Peach Orchard, where Union General Daniel E Sickles advanced his III Corps without orders, thereby creating a salient in the Union line. Sickles lost a leg in the ensuing battle.*

right toward the beleaguered left, the Rebels began moving north down Round Top toward Little Round Top. It was a disastrous prospect for the Army of the Potomac: if Little Round Top were to be taken, the Union left would crumble and Cemetery Ridge would no longer be defensible.

Now the fate of a great battle and of a nation concentrated on a small hill and on the actions of a very few men. One of these men, for a few critical moments the bearer of his nation's destiny, was General Gouverneur K Warren, Meade's chief engineer, who arrived at Little Round Top about this time. To his dismay, Warren saw that this place was the linchpin of the Union position and that there were no troops on it at all, only a signal station. He sent an imperative note to Meade and awaited results while watching Hood's forces – 500 men of the 15th Alabama – climbing toward him.

As bullets began to fly around Warren, a few Federal cannon arrived and began sending canister into the enemy. Then at a run came 350 men of the 20th Maine commanded by young Colonel Joshua Chamberlain, who just one year before had left his position as Professor of Rhetoric at Bowdoin College to realize his dream of becoming a soldier. Now it was up to Chamberlain and the men of Maine to save or lose the Army of the Potomac.

Chamberlain's brigade commander, Colonel Strong Vincent, took him to the southern end of the hill, pointed to the advancing enemy and told Chamberlain to hold the ground at all costs. The 20th Maine spread out in a pitifully thin line, the sparse growth providing little cover. The charging Confederates crashed into the line and began pushing it back. The men of Maine fell in dozens, pulled back, but would not run: the exasperated Confederates could not dislodge

them, even when their guns were in Federal faces. Then Chamberlain saw that his brigade's ammunition was nearly gone. What in God's name was left to do? Dazed and desperate, he ordered the only thing he could think of: "Fix bayonets! Charge bayonets, charge!"

Their bayonets fixed, the men hesitated before this suicidal prospect. Suddenly Lieutenant H S Melcher ran out between the lines, into a hail of bullets, and shouted "Come on! Come on, boys!" Here was another single man on whom the fulcrum of battle swung: the 20th Maine rose from their positions and with a scream of anguish ran right into the Rebels.

The enemy had never seen anything like it (bayonet fighting was in fact rare in the war). In sheer shock, the Confederate line hesitated, then crumbled and ran back downhill. Their confusion was such that one Confederate officer was seen offering his sword in surrender with one hand while firing his pistol with the other. Heading for cover behind a stone wall below, the fleeing Southerners ran head-on into the rifles of the 20th Maine's skirmishers, who had been presumed killed.

For the moment the heroic men of the 20th Maine had saved the Federal left, but General Warren, still on the summit of Little Round Top, saw that the right of Strong Vincent's brigade was caving in. Trying to rally the men, Vincent himself was killed. Warren rode for help and grabbed the first troops he could find, the 140th New York, of Sykes's V Corps, which was now moving up from the rear. Coming up over Little Round Top at a dead run with unloaded guns and no bayonets, the New Yorkers simply charged straight at the enemy, their bodies their only weapons. Somehow this bizarre counterattack worked – the surprised Confederates pulled back. Little Round Top was safe, and Federal soldiers began piling in to reinforce it.

But no one could save the rest of the devastated III Corps. Surrounded by McLaws's men on three sides, Sickles's salient caved in, and McLaws made for the gap that opened

Right: *An attack by Longstreet on the Federal left center.*

Below: *View of Little Round Top, the anchor of the Union left on 2 July*

Above: *At a site called Trostle's Farm, artist C W Reed sketched a Union captain and his men hauling an artillery piece into position by hand.*

up between the fleeing III Corps and Hancock's II Corps. From all over his line, Hancock, ordered by Meade to stop the rout, feverishly rushed troops to plug this gap. Again the battle came down to a few men, this time Union artillerymen around Trostle's Farm. There, just after seven o'clock, Artillery Captain John Bigelow held back William Barksdale's Mississippians long enough for a stronger battery to be mounted to the rear. Fighting surged into the artillery positions, the cannoneers beating back the Rebels with rammers, handspikes and fists; men rolled on the ground slugging away like barroom rowdies. At last Barksdale was killed, and his Mississippians could not get through the gap.

It had been a day of almosts for the Confederacy, but Lee was by no means finished. Southern efforts were shifting steadily northward; the next blow came in the Federal Center on Cemetery Ridge. Hancock, commanding that part of the field, saw a flag moving toward him, apparently from his own lines. He asked angrily why his men were retreating: a volley showed him that it was a Rebel column, some 50 yards away. Hancock rode back and found Colonel Colville of the 1st Minnesota. "Do you see those colours?" Hancock demanded. Colville did. "Well, capture them!" he shouted. Still in marching column, the 1st Minnesota charged the Confederates, who fell back and then rallied, getting the Federals into a pocket. The Minnesotans' line held on somehow, and when the Confederates finally fell back, the 1st Minnesota had 47 men left of the 262 who had charged so gallantly - 82 percent casualties, the worst of the war.

As the fighting began to die down on the center and left, the Confederates settled into position at the base of the Round Tops, in Devil's Den and along the base of Cemetery Ridge. About six in the evening there had been a threat to the Federal right. After an artillery barrage Ewell finally made a move on Culp's Hill, held by Howard's XI Corps. Federal strength there was depleted due to troops being sent south. Edward Johnson's brigade, on the Confederate right, advanced up the hill toward strong but sparsely manned Union breastworks. Again Federal reinforcements arrived in time to stop the attack, and after eight o'clock Johnson's men settled into position on the slopes.

An hour later, in the last fighting of 2 July, Jubal Early's Confederates made it into XI Corps batteries on Cemetery Hill. For the second time that day, Union cannoneers and Rebel infantry fought hand-to-hand, the Union's so-called Dutchmen cursing vigorously in German. After an hour of bitter fighting, Early called it quits when Federal reinforcements arrived for a countercharge. Except for a few confused attempts on Culp's Hill by Ewell's men during the night, the second day's fighting was finally done.

In the middle of the night General Meade took the unusual step of assembling his staff for a council of war. They met in the small shabby farmhouse that was his headquarters. The youngest man attending was General Howard, age 35; Meade, at 45, was the oldest. The Army of the Potomac had lost some 20,000 men in two days of fighting. Now Meade wanted a consensus on what to do next: should they retreat, attack or wait for Lee to attack? The decision was quick and nearly unanimous: they would wait for the Confederate attack. As the generals left, Meade took aside John Gibbon, former commander of the Iron Brigade, who had three brothers in the Southern Army and was to command troops in every remaining major battle of the east. "If Lee attacks tomorrow," Meade told Gibbon, "it will be in your front."

Dawn broke and the Union Army looked out from the heights and waited. Over on the right, at Culp's Hill, there was soon some action. Ewell opened up a cannonade and then sent his men up the hill. But the Federals, in good log-reinforced trenches, turned back the attack with impunity. Then an order from some Union commander went out to scout the Rebel lines a bit; for some reason this reached the 2nd Massachusetts and 27th Indiana as an order for a counterattack. Colonel Charles R Mudge, in command, shrugged "It is murder, but that's the order." He led his two regiments down into the enemy line, and they were cut to pieces, losing a colonel, four color bearers and 250 men, including Colonel Mudge. Following this pointless tragedy another Confederate charge was mounted and broke apart with heavy losses. Ewell finally realized that he had been right, that he could not take Culp's Hill. About 10:30 a silence spread once again over the battlefield.

Again the Union Army waited, resting on their arms. As the morning haze burned off, the day became clear and oppressively hot. Meade tinkered with his dispositions. His lines were still in the shape of a fishhook, Slocum behind in the east and curving to Culp's Hill, Howard from there over to Cemetery Hill, then Gibbon. Hancock (now commanding the III Corps after Sickles's injury), Sykes on the ridge to the

Below: *A painting by Edwin Forbes shows Ewell's Confederates moving toward the sparsely manned Federal position on Culp's Hill on the evening of 2 July.*

Round Tops, Sedgwick and cavalry commander Judson Kilpatrick protecting the left flank.

In the Union middle stood 6000 men of the Second and Third Divisions of the II Corps under Gibbon. The two divisions lay mostly along a stone fence so low the men had to lie or kneel behind it to gain cover. Near the middle of the fence was a little clump of trees, at which point the fence made a dogleg. Behind it were artillery and infantry positioned to fire over the heads of the men in front. It was perhaps the weakest part of the entire Union line.

As the fighting on the right died down, the waiting Federals began to see enemy activity on Seminary Ridge, across the way. Many cannon were being moved into position – a wall of cannon in clear view, their empty muzzles glinting in the late-morning sun as they pointed toward the Union Army. Finally there was a line nearly two miles long, some 150 guns. Opposing them on the Federal side were less than a hundred cannon.

The silence prevailed as noon approached: Hancock opined that the batteries were covering a Confederate retreat. Gibbon was not at all sure about that, but he was sure that he was getting hungry. He invited Meade, Hancock and some other officers to join him behind the II Corps line to reconnoiter a bit of stewed chicken. During lunch Meade shifted Hancock back to his II Corps command and Gibbon to the Second Division. About 12:30 PM Meade excused himself; the others wandered off or lay lolling in the sun.

On the front line dozing Federals sat up and looked across: a puff of smoke was drifting up from one of the Rebel guns. It was one o'clock. Then, pandemonium: all 150 Rebel guns roared at once. The Federal position erupted in a hail of fire and iron. Men died while lighting cigars, with food halfway to their mouths; wagons, trees, horses, men and the very earth itself exploded into the air.

Above: *On 3 July, the last day of fighting at the Battle of Gettysburg, Confederate prisoners are led from the field. Lee had gambled all on a frontal assault.*

Below: *General George E Pickett led his Confederate troops straight into the Union center.*

Right: *"Pickett's Charge."*

The Union guns opened in reply, commanders cautioning their gunners to conserve ammunition. For now it was certain what was happening: this was the prelude to a major assault that would fall where the cannonade was hottest – the II Corps, just as Meade had predicted. Despite the indescribable confusion of men, horses and wagons behind the Federal lines, it became clear that the Confederate gunners were making a fatal mistake – they were firing just a shade too high. As a result, the Union front line, where the coming attack would fall, was scarcely touched.

It went on for an hour and a half, the worst cannonade ever on American soil, and perhaps on any soil to that time. Then slowly it slackened, fell away, died; by three o'clock in the afternoon there was ominous silence again. The men of the II Corps rose to their feet and looked out over the open fields of grain in their front for several minutes. Then they saw something that took their breaths away, something they would never forget: 15,000 of their enemy dressed immaculately on a front half a mile wide and three ranks deep, colors flying, sunlight flashing on musket barrels and drawn swords, officers galloping up and down, the men's steps firm and determined. Silently, the Union men watched their enemy approach. For the last time in the war, perhaps for the last

time in history, it was to be a grand charge in the old Napoleonic style, and it was a terrible and magnificent thing to behold.

That morning Longstreet had struggled for the last time to convince Lee of the necessity for a defensive strategy – a strategic envelopment on the Union right. In reply Lee had pointed imperiously with his fist to Cemetery Hill, saying "The enemy is there, and I am going to strike him." Greatly agitated, Longstreet argued "General, I have been a soldier all my life. It is my opinion that no 15,000 men ever arrayed for battle can take that position." Lee, calm as always, proceeded to give his orders.

While the guns were firing Longstreet had arranged the lines. In front were two divisions, J Johnston Pettigrew on the left and the fresh troops of George E Pickett on the right. To the middle rear was the division of Isaac R Trimble (a mistake in placement, for Trimble was supposed to be in echelon to the left, supporting that flank where fire would be heaviest). Hill and Ewell had been ordered to support the charge, but they did almost nothing.

For some reason history decided to call this action 'Pickett's Charge,' although Longstreet was actually in command. But General George Pickett was certainly one of the

most enthusiastic soldiers on the field. A perfumed dandy, Pickett had been last in his class at West Point, and indeed would probably not have gotten in at all without the influence of his good friend Abraham Lincoln – whose name Pickett would not allow to be slandered in his presence.

On Cemetery Ridge the men of the II Corps watched in awe for a while. Then they got down to business – guns loaded and cocked, thumbs checking the percussion caps, cartridges lined up to hand on the ground. With a running rattle, thousands of muskets stretched out over the stone wall. Lieutenant Alonzo Cushing of Battery 4A, wounded three times in the Rebel cannonade, was being propped by a sergeant amid the wreckage of his battery; his two remaining guns awaited his orders. The Confederate lines marched across half a mile of open fields, the grain parting gently before them; they moved over the plank fences of the Emmitsburg Road, closing in toward the little clump of trees at the angle of the stone wall on Cemetery Ridge. The Federal artillery watched, poised: There, in range! "Fire!"

Now a storm of shell opens into the Rebels. Holes appear in their lines, colors fall and are retrieved. Still the men march steadily forward. They come into shrapnel range, into canister range. Southerners fall in tens, in hundreds; great gaps are torn in the lines. Across the way the Rebel batteries have few shells to fire in reply. The Confederate right flank brushes past some concealed Vermont regiments, who open up a blistering musket fire.

A hundred yards away now. Soon the left side of the Federal line is firing; the Confederates on that flank begin drifting to their left, toward the angle at the little clump of trees. The 8th Ohio, posted forward as skirmishers, enfilades the Confederate left; the flank disappears in smoke. Both Rebel flanks begin to falter, then the left gives way. But the center moves forward still. Pettigrew is down, Generals Garnett and Kemper of Pickett's corps are mortally wounded.

Alonzo Cushing has one gun left; he orders it wheeled down to the stone wall to fire point-blank with triple-shotted canister into the oncoming mass of Rebels. He fires his last

charge just as a fatal bullet finds him. The Rebel spearheard is at the wall now, and some have leaped over it. They are led by General Lewis Armistead, holding his hat on his sword to show his men the way. Armistead is headed for a strange rendezvous with one of his oldest and dearest friends, Winfield Scott Hancock.

Armistead and a handful of men are over the wall; the Rebel colors are arriving one after another; the Rebels are among Cushing's wrecked battery. Armistead himself grasps one of the guns. Gibbon and Hancock are wounded, and Pennsylvanians are retreating from the overrun angle. In this small place and time, the issue is to be decided.

Things happen fast now. The Pennsylvanians rally and surge forward. Reinforcements come from somewhere. A leaderless horde of Federals swarms around the enemy spearhead, while Union cannons continue tearing apart the Rebels in front. Armistead is down, gasping out his life.

All at once, it is finished. The Confederate spearhead seems to dissolve. Some Southerners fall back; others throw down their muskets, raising their hands in surrender. The irresistible charge of a few minutes before becomes a rabble of survivors pouring back down the slope to their own lines.

Meade rides up from the rear, his face very white, and inquires of Lieutenant Franklin Haskell "How is it going here?" "I believe, General, the enemy is repulsed," Haskell replies. "Thank God," Meade says, and adds a choked cheer.

Lying on a stretcher dictating orders, Hancock is interrupted by an aide, who hands him a watch and a few personal effects. They are from Armistead, whose last words were a message to his old friend: "Tell Hancock I have done him and my country a great injustice which I shall never cease to regret." But all regrets are over for Armistead.

Strewn with thousands of dead and wounded, the battleground looked, as one soldier remarked like "a square mile of Tophet." Across the way the beaten Confedeates sank exhausted into their lines, to be visited by Lee who said, and meant it, "All this has been my fault." Even Stuart, finally arrived the previous night, had been repulsed today by Fed-

Left: *Union soldiers relax behind their breastworks on Culp's Hill on 4 July.*

Below: *View from the summit of Little Round Top at 7:30 in the evening of 3 July, as defending Pennsylvania reserves repulse part of Longstreet's corps.*

Opposite: *A Union 12-pounder gun crew, one of the units that helped to repel "Pickett's Charge."*

Overleaf: *A Currier & Ives print depicts Union General Meade (on white horse) commanding at Gettysburg on 3 July.*

Caisson and batt..

Above: *The aftermath of Pickett's Charge.*

Left: *Three Confederate soldiers captured at Gettysburg.*

Below: *Dead Federal soldiers at Gettysburg. Battle casualties were the worst of the war. Lee now withdrew his army slowly back to Virginia.*

eral cavalry on the north flank. For the Army of Northern Virginia it was complte and unmitigated defeat that third of July. A prostrated Pickett wrote to his sweetheart: "My brave boys were so full of hope and confident of victory as I led them forth! Well, it's all over now."

But there was still work to be done. The Confederates next day formed their lines and waited for the counterattack that never came – the Army of the Potomac was too hurt and exhausted for that. In the afternoon of 4 July a downpour began, washing the blood from the grass. Maintaining his lines, Lee buried his dead and evacuated his wounded on a long dismal wagon train that headed back to Virginia. The casualties were the worst of the war: of 88,289 Federals engaged, 3155 were killed, 14,529 wounded - many mortally – and 5365 missing, a total of 23,049 casualties. For the South, of 75,000 engaged, 3903 were killed, 18,735 wounded, 5425 missing, a total of 28,063. Lee had lost over a third of his army.

Reaching the Potomac, the Confederates found the waters swollen and halted on the banks to wait. Meade and his army pursued cautiously, paused before the entrenched enemy but did not attack. Lee's army withdrew across the receding Potomac the night of 13-14 July. Next day there was a rearguard skirmish at Falling Waters, in which Heth lost 500 captured and Pettigrew was killed.

Robert E Lee was a man unaccumstomed to losing, but at Gettysburg he had made the mistake of Napoleon at Wagram and of Burnside at Fredericksburg – throwing a frontal attack against impregnable positions. He had overestimated his army and underestimated his enemy. Now Lee had no choice but to do what Longstreet had begged him to do at the outset – go on the defensive. But first he submitted his resignation to President Davis, assuming full responsibility for the defeat. Davis refused the resignation, knowing that if the South had any hopes at all now, they were in Lee's hands.

Lee had escaped with his army, and thus there was to be more killing, no one knew for how long. Hearing the news of Lee's escape, an anguished Lincoln asked Secretary Welles, "What does it mean? Great God! What does it mean?" A few months later, in his unforgettable words of dedication for the dead at Gettysburg, Lincoln would begin to try and find that meaning.

TOTAL WAR

After the fall of Vicksburg and Lee's calamitous defeat at Gettysburg, the focus of the war shifted to Tennessee, where Union General William S Rosecrans was slowly advancing on the crucial Southern rail center of Chattanooga. By 6 September 1863 Rosecrans had forced his opponent, General Braxton Bragg, to evacuate the city, but Bragg's army was far from finished and, indeed, was planning a deadly surprise for the pursuing Federals. Bragg had established himself in an excellent defensive position a few miles south of Chattanooga, just over the Georgia border, and was rapidly being reinforced. By 19 September, Bragg had achieved numerical superiority and went over to the offense, striking Rosecrans a crushing blow in a wooded area near Chickamauga Creek. Only a dogged delaying action fought on the Union left by General George H Thomas (for which he earned the sobriquet "The Rock of Chickamauga") saved Rosecrans's army from rout, but as it was, Rosecrans was obliged to withdraw into Chattanooga and remain there in a humiliating state of siege until his army was relieved by Grant.

It took Grant a full month of campaigning to repair the damage done at Chickamauga, but he finally did so, the climax coming on 25 November when, in the freakisn Battle of Missionary Ridge, the Confederate line was finally cracked, and Bragg was forced to retire to Dalton, Georgia. The Union was at last in position to mount its long-anticipated offensive into the Deep South.

To be sure, that offensive did not take place until the resumption of campaigning in the spring of 1864, and by then it had become simply one facet of a larger strategic enterprise. Early in 1864 Lincoln had recalled Grant to Washington, had promoted him to lieutenant general (a rank theretofore held only by George Washington) and had placed him in command of all Union armies. In the following weeks Grant had evolved a massive, potentially war-winning strategy involving simultaneous advances on five separate fronts. William Tecumseh Sherman, who now had Grant's old job of commanding the Western armies, would strike into Georgia. George Meade and the Army of the Potomac, under Grant's personal supervision, would at the same time drive due south towards Richmond. To these major offensives would be added three lesser ones in the Virginia Peninsula, the Shenandoah Valley and Alabama. In the event, all three of the small offensives would fail, and the entire burden would be carried by Sherman and Grant alone.

The multiple Union offensive began on 4 May 1864, and Grant's part of it was quickly embroiled in savage fighting with Lee's Army of Northern Virginia. Time and again Lee tried to break Grant's momentum – in The Wilderness, at Spotsylvania, at North Anna and at Cold Harbor – and each time, after a bloody confrontation, Grant would disengage, slide around to the right and continue his relentless advance. By 18 June he was actually south of Richmond, facing Lee's heavily fortified positions at Petersburg, the major rail junction supplying the Confederate capital. At this point Grant abandoned maneuver and settled in for a long siege. Thus far, casualties on both sides in the Eastern Theater had been appalling: 50,000 (41 percent) for the Union and 32,000 (46 percent) for the Confederacy.

At the same time U S Grant was setting out to challenge Robert E Lee in the East, the other part of the Union's grand strategy was rolling into motion in the South. Grant's closest associate in the army, William Tecumseh Sherman, had been ordered "to move against Johnston's army, to break it up, and to get into the interior of the enemy's country as far as you can, inflicting all the damage you can against their war resources."

Sherman's forces, now consisting of three entire armies, lay in Chattanooga. They were the Army of the Cumberland under "Rock of Chickamauga" George H Thomas; the Army of the Tennessee under James B McPherson; and the Army of the Ohio under John M Schofield – in all, over 100,000 men. Their immediate goal was the critical supply, manufacturing

Left: *Union troops move against massed Confederates in the Wilderness on 5 May 1864.*

and communications center of Atlanta, Georgia, some 140 miles to the southwest.

Sherman's opponent would be General Joseph E Johnston, whose Confederate Army of Tennessee lay south of Chattanooga in Dalton, Georgia. President Jefferson Davis had reluctantly given that command to Johnston after a public clamor following the defeat at Chattanooga had forced the removal of Davis's friend, the incompetent Braxton Bragg. Despite his differences with Davis, Johnston was one of the best generals the South had, and he defined his present goals clearly. He had only 62,000 men and therefore could not immediately take the offensive, especially when the Federals were led by one as able as Sherman. Thus Johnston's tactics must be defensive, resisting Sherman on every foot of ground, forcing him to overextend his supply line and reduce his forces to protect it. When they were reduced, it would be time to take the offensive. Finally, *Atlanta must not fall before*

the presidential election. In sum, Johnston realized his strategy must be Fabian – a fighting retirement over successive positions. This would weaken Sherman for the kill and make it likely that a more accommodating Union president could be elected.

There were two major problems with implementing Johnston's strategy. One was Jefferson Davis, the other a member of his own staff – General John B Hood, who hated defensive strategy of any kind. The army's other generals – William J Hardee, Leonidas Polk and cavalry leader Joseph Wheeler – would wait and see. As for the Army of Tennessee itself, it was

Below: *Sherman's March to the Sea from Atlanta split the Confederacy in two along an east-west axis.*

Bottom: *Sherman's Atlanta Campaign, beginning with his departure from Chattanooga 4 May.*

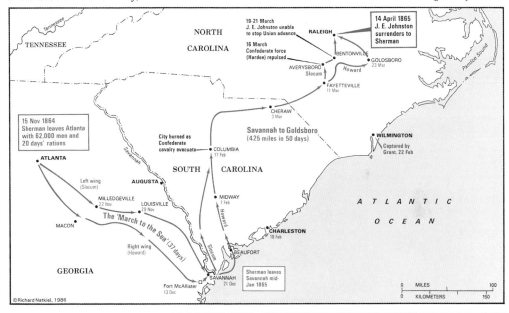

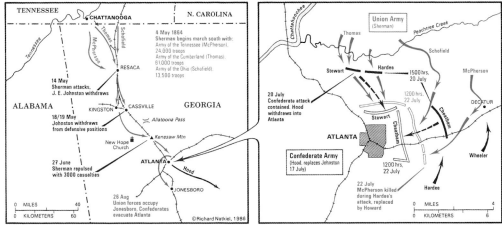

Left: *William Tecumseh Sherman surrounded by commanders of the Union armies in the West.*

MAJ.GEN.J.M.SCHOFIELD.

MAJ.GEN.G.H.THOMAS.

MAJ.GEN.J.B.McPHERSON.

MAJ.GEN.H.W.SLOCUM.

MAJ.GEN.W.T.SHERMAN.

MAJ.GEN.O.O.HOWARD.

MAJ.GEN.A.H.TERRY.

MAJ.GEN.W.S.ROSECRANS.

MAJ.GEN.E.R.S.CANBY.

Eng.^d by H.B.Hall Jr.

UNION GENERALS.

Opposite top: *Battlefield at Resaca, Georgia, one of nine successive defensive positions Johnston would yield as his forces fell back toward Atlanta.*

Opposite bottom: *The wreckage of a train derailed by Confederate irregulars is examined by Union engineers.*

in splendid condition, its equipment and spirit restored by Johnston after the humiliation at Chattanooga.

On 7 May 1864 Sherman's great offensive got under way, his troops probing Confederate positions around Dalton. That morning, as Union troops clashed with the enemy near Ringgold, Georgia, a Federal officer observed "The ball is opened." The ensuing campaign to Atlanta was indeed to be like a formal dance, Sherman sweeping to the side of his opposite, Johnston gracefully withdrawing.

On 9 May McPherson's Federal Army flanked Johnston and gained his rear at Snake Creek Gap, threatening Confederate communications at Resaca. On 12 May the Confederates pulled back to strong entrenchments around Resaca, where

Sherman mounted three futile attacks against the Rebel lines. At the same time he sent other forces around Johnston's left flank. This dislodged the Confederates three days later. Retiring without haste, the Confederate Army of Tennessee came to a halt farther south at Cassville.

So the dance progressed, sashaying southeast around the fulcrum of the Western and Atlantic Railroad toward Atlanta. The Rebels would break up the railroad as they withdrew, the Yankees would repair it as they advanced. From positions at Cassville, Johnston prepared to mount an attack but was dissuaded by Hood and Polk, who claimed they were flanked. The Confederates then withdrew briefly to Allatoona but found Sherman brushing by their left. Sending Wheeler's

cavalry to raid Sherman's ever-lengthening supply line, Johnston moved west to positions near Dallas, where beginning on 25 May there was a sharp fight that lasted four days. On the first and third days Sherman assaulted the Confederate entrenchments and lost heavily. On 4 June, however, Johnston realized Sherman was again flanking his left and pulled back to prepared positions at Kennesaw Mountain, near Marietta. Sherman followed and the dance continued; thus far it had accounted for some 9000 casualties on each side.

Sherman knew well that every step he took made his supply line more tenuous. In early June his cavalry moved east and again secured the railroad, which improved his prospects. (The Civil War was the first in history wherein railroads were essential in moving men and supplies.) But there were threats to Federal supply lines farther back, in Tennessee and Mississippi, centered in the person of Confederate cavalryman Nathan Bedford Forrest, an almost illiterate former slave-trader who had become one of the most brilliant and aggressive generals of the war.

Sherman declared, with his customary ferocity, "That devil Forrest . . . must be hunted down and killed if it costs ten thousand lives and bankrupts the Federal Treasury." In early June Federal cavalry under General S D Sturgis were dispatched to deal with Forrest. In his finest action, commanding less than half Sturgis's numbers, Forrest completely routed the Federals and inflicted enormous losses at Brice's Crossroads, Mississippi (10 May). Union efforts to hunt down "that devil" were to continue, and to fail, right to the war's end. Nonetheless, Sherman's supplies were never seriously disrupted.

By 14 June Sherman's men were in sight of Johnston's positions on Kennesaw Mountain. That day a Federal artillery bat-

Below: *The start of General Sherman's doomed frontal assault on Johnston's Rebels well-entrenched on Kennesaw Mountain near Marietta, Georgia.*

tery lobbed a few cannonballs at a Confederate staff conference on Pine Mountain, one of which squarely caught General Polk, killing him instantly. Sherman had only to flank Johnston again to destroy the position. But for some reason, perhaps partly in order to vary his tactics, Sherman decided on an assault. He sent his men sharply uphill into strong works fronted by abatis and swept by crossfire. The result, on 27 June, was a debacle. "All that was necessary," one Rebel defender wrote, "was to load and shoot." The Federals suffered over 2000 casualties to the South's 442. Yet Sherman scarcely paused to lick his wounds. In a few days he sent McPherson east around Johnston's right flank toward the Chattahoochie River, just northwest of Atlanta.

Failing to anticipate this move was Johnston's first mistake in the campaign. As a result, he was forced to withdraw to the banks of the Chattahoochie, knowing he could not remain there long and that the next stop was Atlanta. This was not his only problem – an increasingly frustrated Davis was pressing him to take the offensive: Johnston was caught between a still impregnable enemy on one side and an implacable commander-in-chief on the other.

On 17 July a telegram arrived from Davis relieving Johnston and giving command of the Army of Tennessee to General John B. Hood. It was in essence an order to attack, which was what Hood would certainly do. Sherman was delighted.

Sherman's three armies converged on Atlanta. Lulled by token resistance, Sherman speculated that Hood, contrary to form, might be evacuating the city. He sent McPherson's army away on a wide envelopment to the east, heading for Hood's rail line. The Federals became careless. On the afternoon of 20 July, Thomas was moving his army slowly across Peachtree Creek; there was a gap of several miles between his army and those of Schofield and McPherson. It was a serious oversight, but after all, the enemy was supposed to be retreating. In the afternoon the men were resting on the banks of the creek.

Above: *Pencil sketch by A R Waud of Sherman (astride the horse facing right) at Kennesaw Mountain.*

Right: *Wash drawing by A R Waud of the Federal artillery bombarding Kennesaw Mountain.*

Then Hood struck and struck hard, his forces swarming on to the surprised Federals. There was a fierce four-hour fight at close quarters; the Rebels moved around Thomas's right flank, into the gap in the Federal line. For the Federals there was no time to hope for reinforcements. Across the creek, "Rock of Chickamauga" Thomas found some reserve batteries and began shelling the Confederates along the opposite bank. In Thomas's phrase, that cannonade "relieved the hitch"; the Rebels fell back. Thomas's men had proved as good as their leader. Both sides had had about 20,000 engaged; Confederate losses were some 4800 to about 1800 for the Union. Hood's aggressive strategy thus had a most inauspicious beginning. But the Rebel general was by no means ready to relinquish the initiative, such as it was. Hearing that McPherson's left flank was exposed east of Atlanta and a Federal wagon train vulnerable at Decatur, Hood moved to attack again. While the main body of the Confederates fell back to fortifications around Atlanta, Wheeler was ordered to take his cavalry to Decatur and Hardee to march 15 miles to attack McPherson's flank at dawn. Thus came about the Battle of Atlanta on 22 July.

That morning Hood waited anxiously for the sounds of Hardee's attack. Finally, at about 11:00 AM, he heard skirmishers open up on the Union left – but apparently in front of McPherson's line, not on the flank as ordered. Hood was furious at this apparent blunder. When Hardee's attack began, Sherman and McPherson were conferring in the middle of the Federal position. Puzzled by the unexpected sound of firing on his front, McPherson leaped on to his horse

to investigate. Sherman paced nervously, waiting for news. Shortly an aide dashed up and reported that McPherson's horse had returned bleeding and riderless. McPherson had found Hardee's attack hitting hard, but their attempt to flank him had run afoul of Grenville Dodge's XVI Corps, which was moving into position on the left when the Rebels charged. Thus Hardee had moved as ordered on the enemy flank, but when he got there it was no longer a flank. Dodge's men were pushed back in furious fighting, but put up enough resistance to blunt the attack. McPherson had arrived just in time to see a successful countercharge by Ohio regiments. He then dressed his lines and headed to the right to see how the XVII Corps was faring.

McPherson rode right into a group of Confederate skirmishers, who signaled him to surrender. In response, he politely tipped his hat and bolted; immediately he was shot

dead from his horse. When his body was brought to Sherman, the general wept openly; at 35 McPherson had been one of the brightest and most promising generals in the army. Command of the Army of the Tennessee was given to General Oliver O Howard, a one-armed veteran of Chancellorsville and Gettysburg.

The battle on the Union left was to rage furiously into the evening, but Hardee's men made no headway after their first assault. The Yankees were as determined as their attackers, sometimes meeting and repelling simultaneous attacks on front and rear. Farther to the east, Wheeler had no better luck in his assault on Decatur.

Bitterly disappointed by the lack of success on the Federal left, Hood sent General Benjamin Cheatham's corps to attack the center of the Union line at three o'clock in the afternoon. The Confederates charged to the east along a railroad and

Left: *A Union cavalryman examines recently taken fortifications at Atlanta.*

Above: *John B Hood replaced Johnston on 17 July 1864.*

punched clear through the Union center, capturing two batteries. But in the end, they too were driven back by Union artillery.

For the second time Hood had failed. His casualties were some 8000 of nearly 37,000 engaged, to the North's 3722 of 30,000 engaged. The Confederates had fought the best they knew how, with superior numbers, and failed. It would take as good a general as Sherman to whip the Federals, but Hood knew only how to fight, not how to make plans.

After the battle Atlanta was besieged. On 28 July Sherman ordered Howard's army to cut the railroad to the south. Hood sent the corps of S D Lee against Howard at Ezra Church; six Rebel assault waves could not rout them but did succeed in keeping the railroad open to Atlanta. Sherman steadily tightened his grip around the city, meanwhile sending more futile sorties against Forrest in Mississippi. He now had command

of all the rail lines into Atlanta except the Macon line to the south. In late July 10,000 cavalry under Edward McCook and George Stoneman were sent to raid Macon and cut the railroad. Sherman learned thereby that Hood was still dangerous: McCook's division was routed and dispersed, Stoneman's all but wiped out. For the moment, the Confederates' lifeline stayed open.

In mid-August Hood took the offensive again, making one of the most serious in the chain of blunders that had shattered and demoralized his army. Wheeler's cavalry was ordered to raid Sherman's supply line to the north. The raid lasted a month, but Sherman had already collected all the supplies he needed, and the absence of cavalry fatally weakened Confederate defenses in Atlanta. That fact was not lost on Sherman, who had been waiting for Hood to make the ultimate mistake. This was it.

Leaving a small force before the city, Sherman pulled the armies of Schofield and Thomas from their trenches on 26 August and made a wide sweep around the west of Atlanta, heading for the Macon rail line to the south. Hood concluded the enemy was giving up. Telegrams went out all over the Confederacy: "The Yankees are gone!" Several railway cars full of ladies arrived in town to assist in the celebration. Hood sent troops south to Jonesboro to hasten his enemy's retreat, but by the end of the 31st the Federals had easily repelled that force and cut the railroad in two places.

Obtuse as he was, Hood knew the game was up. On 1 September he evacuated Atlanta, blowing up the munitions and stores he could not carry away and heading for entrenchments to the southwest at Lovejoy. On the next day the Federals roared into the city, and Sherman telegraphed Lincoln "Atlanta is ours, and fairly won." The overjoyed president declared a national day of celebration for the victories at Atlanta and Mobile Bay. Privately, he celebrated his own suddenly improved prospects for re-election.

Sherman now decided on a course of action that would make him simultaneously one of the great generals of history and the most hated personage in the long memory of the South. He decreed that the full weight of war was to fall on the civilians of the Confederacy. Atlanta was to become a military camp, its population forcibly evacuated, all buildings of possible military importance destroyed. (Ultimately, only half the civilians were evacuated, and his men were ordered not to burn private dwellings, but they often got a little careless with matches: no one was likely to stop them.) Sherman wrote to Halleck, "If the people raise a howl against my barbarity and cruelty, I will answer that war is war, and not popularity seeking. If they want peace, they and their relations must stop the war."

Hood was soon on the road again with his army, heading north to operate against Sherman's supply line in a desperate gamble to force a Federal retreat. First sending Thomas's army to Nashville on 3 October, Sherman set out in pursuit of Hood, following him back north along his old route. Again Kennesaw Mountain, Allatoona, Resaca and Chattanooga echoed to the sound of gunfire. Then Sherman came to rest in Kingston, Georgia, and made an historic change of plans. He decided to let Hood go, to let Schofield and Thomas handle him. Hood could not stop him now: Sherman would set out on a gamble of his own. As he and Grant had done in Mississippi on the way to Jackson, he would cut his supply line and march away from Hood, directly across Georgia to the sea. He would show the South and the world that his 60,000 men could go anywhere in enemy territory with impunity. On

the way he would take what food his army needed from the people. He would destroy the South's will to resist, would "make Georgia howl."

"War," Shermon wrote, "like the thunderbolt, follows its own laws and turns not aside even if the beautiful, the virtuous and the charitable stand in its path." At the time, this was considered barbarism; future generations would call it Total War.

Thus Sherman left Hood to his desperate and ineffectual raids and moved back to Atlanta to complete the work of destruction. On 16 November he set out to the east across the South toward Savannah and the sea. As far as the world was concerned he marched into a hole: there would be no communication. His army was ordered not only to forage off the land but to "enforce a devastation more or less relentless." With the air of a holiday rather than a campaign, his army made about ten miles a day and spread aross a front some 50 miles wide. That front cut through the South like a scythe, leaving a burning and ravaged swath across the rich landscape. On the periphery, like a swarm of locusts, ranged a rabble of deserters – both Yankees and Rebels bonded by a common rapacity. These "bummers," as they were called, robbed and burned at random. Opposing Sherman's march was a motley collection of state militias and Wheeler's cavalry – some 13,000 in all. Though they forced the Federals to contend with almost constant skirmishing, they could not begin to halt their progress.

Meanwhile, Hood continued haplessly on his way north in Tennessee, battering his army to pieces on the Federal juggernaut. On 30 November he lost 6000 men in attacking Schofield at Franklin. He continued somehow to Nashville, where in mid-December Thomas finally wrecked what little was left of the Confederate Army of Tennessee, which had been

Right: *S D Lee's Rebels attacking General Oliver Howard's army at Ezra Church on 28 July. Six assaults failed to dislodge the Federal troops.*

Below: *An Atlanta railroad station after occupation by Federal troops. It is being used as a staging area; note the troops atop the boxcars and the tents in the background.*

hounded to death by President Davis's almost unerring facility for firing good generals and promoting bad ones.

On December 10 the world learned that Sherman had emerged unscathed at Savannah. Three days later the Rebel fort outside the city fell; Hardee, in command, evacuated the city on the 21st. Sherman facetiously wired to Lincoln, "I beg to present you, as a Christmas gift, the city of Savannah." The March to the Sea was accomplished. Sherman prepared to turn north through the Carolinas to join Grant's Army; together they would finish off Lee. The march through the Carolinas was to be another campaign of destruction.

William Tecumseh Sherman had fulfilled his task, had mortally wounded the Confederacy's potential for war, had earned the unbridled admiration of the North and the undying hatred of the South. Was his ruthlessness justifiable? History has debated that issue ever since.

On paper, Sherman was ferocious – his letters bristle with threats: "I shall then feel justified in resorting to the harshest measures, and shall make little effort to restrain my army"; "Until we can re-populate Georgia, it is useless to occupy it, but the utter destruction of its roads, homes, and people will cripple their military resources"; "I almost tremble for her [South Carolina's] fate." Yet none of these threats came fully to pass. By modern standards, his campaign was scarcely a reign of terror at all, since most of the violence and looting fell on property, not persons. There was none of the indiscriminate slaughter of modern guerrilla war and terrorism.

In the end it could be argued that Sherman was not the real culprit in the March to the Sea, that the true blame lies in the fact put forth succinctly by Sherman himself in the statement: "War is hell." From the Civil War onward, that judgment would resonate ever more deeply.

PETERSBURG

By the summer of 1864, the Confederacy was sinking into defeat. It had lost most of its vital cities and ports, a substantial number of its men and its grip on the oppressive slave-labor system that had supported its economy. Already there was serious talk of enlisting freed slaves in the Confederate Army, which was a manifestly desperate course. (In the North the Thirteenth Amendment, abolishing slavery as an institution, was in preparation.)

Yet the Rebels fought on. The Union Army of the Potomac had been hard hit in the Wilderness, at Spotsylvania and at Cold Harbor. When U S Grant changed his tactics in June, ordering his army south, away from Richmond, it was partly an admission of short-term frustration and partly an assumption of victory in the long run. He would besiege Petersburg, a rail center through which flowed the food and supplies Lee's army lived and fought on. When Petersburg fell, both Richmond and Lee would be finished, and so would the last hope of the Confederacy.

As at Vicksburg, Grant had begun by trying to avoid a siege, but was forced to settle for the inevitable. The main Confederate entrenchments surrounded Petersburg in a large east-west arc, both ends resting on the Appomattox River, which was protected against Union ships by cannon. Grant's lines took shape to the east, and over the next months slowly crept to the west around the city. On 22-23 July the Federals made a sortie against the Weldon Railroad south of Petersburg, but A P Hill's men pushed them back. Meanwhile, Confederate General Jubal Early had mounted a raid toward Washington that threw the capital into a panic and brought his forces to the very gates of the city before he fell back on 11 July. Early's purpose, of course, was to draw away Grant's men from Petersburg. Knowing, or at least hoping, that Washington was strong enough, Grant did not take the bait. Lee was his only objective.

There was another Federal offensive around Petersburg during July, one that would cap the military career of the

Left: *A lithograph entitled "Come and Join Us Brothers" published by the Supervisory Committee for Recruiting Colored Regiments in Philadelphia. About 186,000 blacks served on both sides.*

Below: *Confederate soldiers at Petersburg prepare for the Union siege.*

Opposite: *A pencil drawing by Edwin Forbes shows the Union 18th Corps storming the first line of fortifications outside of Petersburg on 14 June 1864.*

genial and inept Ambrose E Burnside. Burnside's fancy had been caught by one Colonel Henry Pleasants, who had been a mining engineer before the war. Pleasants had formulated a plan to dig a 510-foot tunnel under the Confederate trenches at Elliot's Salient, just east of the city. Grant and Meade were distinctly cool to the notion, but approved it mainly to keep Burnside and his men out of trouble. On 25 June, 400 Pennsylvania coal miners went to work. By 23 July the tunnel, of unprecedented length in military history, was completed, and workers began placing hundreds of barrels of black powder in magazines dug under the Confederate parapets. Burnside had not neglected to prepare troops for this unusual duty. The division of General Edward Ferrero had spent a month training for the attack. They had been picked supposedly because they were the freshest troops in the army. They also happened to be a black division.

Black troops had been actively recruited in the North since 1863; by the end of the war they numbered about 300,000, many of them former slaves. Their progress in the Union Army had been attended by all the racism then prevalent in the North as well as the South. Their fighting ability had been maligned, until they had repeatedly proved they could fight as well as whites (their officers were almost entirely white). In the army they remained a touchy subject, a problem close to the core of the entire American dilemma.

On 30 July the show was ready to begin. However, on the day before, Meade, with Grant's approval, had ordered a change in plans: the black division was not to lead the attack – if it failed, public opinion might accuse the Union of callously misusing its black soldiers (which, given the experimental nature of the operation, was very possibly the case). After this rebuff, Burnside seemed listless and indifferent, simply drawing straws to see whose division would lead the attack. James H Ledlie, commanding the I Division, lost. Burnside must have known this was the weakest division in the army and Ledlie the least experienced general, but it did not seem to bother him. Furthermore, Burnside was vague in giving his final instructions: Ledlie rounded up his men with only a very hazy idea of what they were supposed to do.

The explosion was planned for 3:30 in the morning on the 30th. At that moment all eyes strained toward the Rebel parapet. Ledlie's division waited in the trenches, but nothing happened. It was discovered that the long fuse had fizzled, and it was relit. At 4:45 AM one of the largest explosions ever seen on the American continent sent flames, earth, cannons, Confederates and parts of Confederates a hundred feet into the air in the midst of a mushroom-shaped cloud. When it had all settled, there was a gigantic crater 170 feet long, 60 to 80 feet wide and 30 feet deep stretching well into the Southern position, the outer defenses of which had been breached.

For the time being, the surviving Rebel defenders had fled the area. Terrified by the blast, so had Ledlie's division. It took ten minutes to get them back in position to advance, at

Below: *Drawing by Alfred R Waud for* Harper's Weekly *showing the explosion of the mine at Petersburg on 30 July. The stratagem proved disastrous for the Union soldiers.*

which point it was discovered that no provision at all had been made to get them out of the trenches, which were quite deep. They scrambled up as best they could, already considerably disorganized, and then stopped around the crater to gawk at the appalling mess within. With some prodding, the I Division began jumping and sliding into the hole. Finding themselves in a morass of pits and house-high blocks of clay, they stumbled in confusion toward the other end. Meanwhile Ledlie, their commander, cowered in a bombproof shelter behind Union lines, consoled by a jug of rum.

Soon the Southerners collected their wits and began to train their artillery and muskets into the hole. Finding themselves relatively sheltered in the crater, the ostensible attackers were even less disposed to climb out of it. By the time 15,000 men had been herded into the crater, the enemy fire had become truly murderous and the Federals were interested solely in hiding. The Union Army was now literally at the feet of the enemy.

Finally, in desperation, Burnside ordered in the black division originally slated to lead the attack. After dispatching them, their commander, Ferrero, joined Ledlie in the bombproof shelter. The black soldiers advanced resolutely and alone and were cut to pieces on the other end, though not before somehow taking 250 prisoners. Firing into the huddled masses of Federals, the Confederates screamed, "Take the white man – kill the nigger!" The whole inglorious affair ended with a confused melee of surviving Federals rushing devil-take-the-hindmost back to their own lines. The North suffered 3748 casualties of 20,708 engaged – about a third of them from the black division; the South lost about 1500 of 11,466.

Grant called the Petersburg mine assault a "stupendous failure," while admitting that if the black troops had led the attack as planned it would probably have succeeded. Lincoln's reported reaction was an historic epitaph to the unique military career of Ambrose E Burnside: "Only Burn-

Above: *Artillery battery of the Union 18th Corps at a captured fort on the outer line at Petersburg on 15 June, 1864.*

Left: *Officers and men of the 114th Pennsylvania Infantry relax in front of Petersburg in August 1864.*

Overleaf: *The "Dictator," a 13-inch siege mortar used in the bombardment of Richmond and Petersburg.*

side could have managed such a coup, wringing one last spectacular defeat from the jaws of victory."

The siege of Petersburg continued, day on day, month on month. In its first weeks there had been no rain, and a choking cloud of dust hung everywhere. Later weeks brought too much rain; the men in the trenches stood all day in waist-high water. Snipers waited in readiness for those careless enough to show their heads. Every day a battle raged somewhere; cannon and mortars roared incessantly (the soldiers hated the mortars most – they could drop shells unexpectedly straight into the trenches). The Federals gradually inched around the city, moving steadily toward the Confederate lifelines of the railroads.

The Army of the Potomac was hardly the same force that had set out in May. Subjected to three months of the hardest and most deadly fighting in American history, it had lost well over half its veterans in casualties over the summer of 1864. Many famous units, like the Iron Brigade, had virtually ceased to exist. The fabled II Corps, which began the summer with 6799 men, had suffered 7970 casualties, including 40 regimental commanders. Yet that corps and the whole army stayed more or less at strength, thanks largely to the draft and to enlistment bounties that kept personnel in the trenches but by no means guaranteed good soldiers. And the sullen waiting and ducking of trench warfare was poor training for an army of recruits.

The rigors of the campaign and the siege had their effect on the Northern command structure as well. Meade was more irascible than ever, and his relations with Grant – which so far had been surprisingly good – began to deteriorate to the extent that Grant considered relieving him. Hancock, the best fighting general in the army, was troubled and demoralized by his old Gettysburg wound and by the strain of constant fighting; he quarreled with John Gibbon, his best division commander.

Lee's troops were also devastated, and hungrier and shabbier than ever. They were nearly all veterans, for the simple reason that there were few recruits to be found. For all their experience, however, hunger, exhaustion, disease and desertion had taken their toll. The army was by no means capable of the heroics of its recent past; indeed, it was hardly capable of taking the offensive at all. The weight of the North was slowly squeezing the life out of the Army of Northern Virginia, the South's only remaining viable army.

In August of 1864, Grant sent General Gouverneur K Warren to try again to seize the Weldon Railroad south of Petersburg. The Federals occupied the line on the 18th, and two attacks by A P Hill could not dislodge them, though the North had 4455 casualties to the South's 1600. Now only one Confederate lifeline was left – the South Side Railroad on the west.

In September Grant sent "Phil" Sheridan with infantry and cavalry on a campaign into the Shenandoah Valley of Virginia, which would become nearly as famous as Stonewall Jackson's operations there in 1862. Sheridan had two goals. First, he was to drive out Jubal Early, whose army had retired there after the raid on Washington. Second, he was to make quite sure the valley would send no more food and forage to Confederate Armies. Grant's instructions were ruthless: devastation was to be so complete that a crow flying over the valley would have to carry its own provisions.

Sheridan proceeded to turn the fertile, beautiful Shenandoah Valley into a smouldering ruin. In the process he dealt harshly with Jubal Early, defeating him at Winchester and Fisher's Hill in mid-September. On 19 October Early's men suddenly attacked and routed the Federals at Cedar Creek while Sheridan was away. Arriving and riding furiously through his fleeing troops, Sheridan turned them around and swamped Early's army. It was the last significant Rebel resistance in the valley, which had been the breadbasket of the Confederacy.

Sheridan then pursued his course through the Shenandoah Valley like an avenging angel. A small but volatile man of manic ferocity in battle, Sheridan drove his men and officers almost as hard as he drove the enemy. An admiring sub-

*Opposite: Surgeons'
quarters at the camp of the
50th New York Engineers in
front of Petersburg in
November, 1864.*

*Right: Abandoned
Confederate field defenses of
earth and timber around
Petersburg.*

*Below: Part of the Union
lines outside Petersburg.*

ordinate called him "that form of condensed energies"; to the Rebels, he was "Sheridan the Inevitable."

On 8 November Abraham Lincoln was re-elected to a second term as president by a substantial majority over his opponent, General George B McClellan. Significantly, for all their affection for "Little Mac," the military vote went overwhelmingly to Lincoln. The doubts felt by many civilians in the North about the president's war policy were clearly not shared by the army.

In mid-January 1865, after a bungled attempt by Ben Butler that got him fired, Admiral David Dixon Porter took Fort Fisher on the coast of North Carolina, the last port held by the Confederacy for its blockade-runners and virtually its last link to the outside world. Now the South was alone.

In February Grant extended his lines to Hatcher's Run, south of Petersburg. Sherman, meanwhile, was fighting and burning his way north through the Carolinas toward union with the Army of the Potomac. If Sherman effected that union, Lee's army had not a chance in the world. Shattered and tired as the Confederates were, they had to try something; the only choices left were those of desperation.

At length Lee decided to try and get part of his army to Carolina to join forces with Joe Johnston, who was incapable of resisting Sherman alone. Perhaps together they could deal with Sherman and then turn to defeat Grant.

The Southern attempt to break out of Petersburg came on 25 March at Ford Stedman, east of the city. Lying 150 yards from the Confederate position, it was the weakest part of the Federal line. Lee hoped to break through here and strike the Federal communications, thereby forcing Grant to pull troops from farther south and leave an opening in his line through which Lee could send forces south to Johnston. In the early morning, Federals at Fort Stedman were surprised and quickly overwhelmed by the Confederates; the Rebel infantry was swarming down the Union trenches and into the Federal rear before any resistance was mounted. For an hour or so it seemed like old times. But then a counterattack by six new Pennsylvania regiments, commanded by General John Hartranft, brought the Confederate advance to a halt. At eight o'clock Lee called off the attack. It was the last great offensive of the Army of Northern Virginia. The next day Lee notified President Davis that his position in Petersburg was no longer

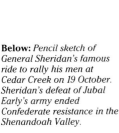

door. Robert E Lee was far from a loser, but he had lost. His ranks and his command structure were decimated: Jackson, Stuart, dozens of other generals were dead. The Army of Northern Virginia had been one of the most remarkable fighting forces in history, but it had lost. Now it had only to play out its role to the final curtain.

The curtain came down with bewildering speed. On 29 March Grant sent cavalry and infantry under Sheridan and Warren southwest to envelop the Confederate right flank. Lee dispatched 10,000 men under George Pickett to stop them. The Federal operation was slowed by heavy rains and Rebel resistance, but Sheridan was implacable: vowing the rain would not stop his cavalry, he shouted, "I'm ready to strike out tomorrow and go to smashing things!"

On 31 March, Sheridan assaulted Pickett around Dinwiddie Court House; outnumbered five to one, Pickett's force fought for hours before pulling back to Five Forks. Lee sent a desperate message to Pickett to hold that position "at all costs"; if it fell, the South Side Railroad, the last lifeline, was doomed. But on 1 April Sheridan, seemingly everywhere on the field at once with his battle flag, overpowered the Confederates at Five Forks and captured nearly half of them. Many of the rest fled the war back to their homes.

Now Lee had to get out. He notified Davis on 2 April that he would evacuate Petersburg. Grant, determined above all else not to let Lee escape again, unleashed a stupendous artillery barrage on the whole length of the Confederate line, and followed it with an attack by the VI Corps, who broke through the Rebel right. In the fighting, A P Hill, who had saved the Confederacy at Antietam and had been at Lee's side through all the victories, was killed. The news visibly staggered Lee.

During the day the Confederate Government fled Richmond. Warehouses and arsenals were set afire, the flames spreading into the city. Lee pulled out that night and marched his exhausted and starving army west toward Amelia Court House, hoping to put them on the Danville Railroad to the Carolinas. On 3 April Federal soldiers occupied Petersburg and Richmond. The next day the Confederate capital saw the lanky form of Abraham Lincoln, surrounded by cheering slaves, striding through the streets. At last Lincoln sat pondering at the desk of Jefferson Davis.

If defeat seemed incredible to the Confederate Army, the

tenable, given the approach of Sherman, and that the Confederate Government had best consider pulling out of Richmond. Simultaneously, Sheridan's Federal forces arrived back from their devastation of the Shenandoah Valley, ready to join in the last battle.

For Robert E Lee, for the Army of Northern Virginia, for the Confederate States of America, the incredible was about to happen. After all the glorious speeches, the fatuous defenses of slavery, the gallant fighting and the victories, the unforeseen and terrible suffering and dying – after all this, the gaunt and humiliating specter of final defeat was at their

Left: *An attempt to take the defenses outside Petersburg. The city was finally occupied by Union troops on 3 April 1865.*

Below: *Sketch of railroad cars and workshops burned by the Rebels evacuating Petersburg.*

prospect of victory after so many disappointments was equally incredible to Union soldiers. News of the fall of Richmond was received by Union troops at first with derision: they had heard that one before. No sooner had they absorbed the reality than they were on the road in the final race with the enemy. Sheridan had anticipated Lee's march to Amelia Court House and rode to cut off the Danville Railroad. Lee's army was now surrounded – Meade's infantry was on the east and Sheridan on the south and west. Escape to the north was impossible. Lee the fox was being run to earth by Sheridan the hound. Rebel soldiers were deserting in hundreds. "My God!," cried Lee, "Is the army dissolved?"

Denied the railroad by Sheridan, Lee marched again on 5 April. By the next day his army was divided by accident into two segments. Led by Sheridan's dismounted cavalry, the Federals fell on one of the wings at Saylor's Creek and captured 8000, one-third of the remaining Rebel strength. The pathetic remains of the Army of Northern Virginia limped on to the west, harried incessantly by Federal cavalry. Then on 9 April Lee found sheridan the Inevitable blocking his path at Appomattox Court House. It was the end.

But still the shadow of that great army could not die without a fight. Lee sent cavalry around the Federal right flank, and infantry and artillery under John B Gordon broke through the center of Sheridan's line. For a brief moment there was open country in front of the Army of Northern Virginia. Then from over the hill appeared Union infantry, line after line of blue.

The firing died down. For the last time the two armies surveyed one another across the battlefield. Then Sheridan sounded his bugles for the charge. But before the Federals could fall upon the ragged Confederates, a horseman appeared, galloping furiously from behind Southern lines. He carried a white flag.

The war was over, and it was not over. Lee's surrender to Grant at Appomattox on 9 April almost ended the hostilities (Johnston surrendered to Sherman on the 18th). But the assassination of Lincoln on 14 April was only the first of the aftershocks that would shake American society: the Civil War would never leave the consciousness of the nation.

Lincoln above all had tried to see beyond the immediate business and horror of the war to the deeper questions: What good could come out of this suffering? What did it all mean?

Above: *A Mathew Brady photo of the ruins of Richmond, burned by its defenders on 2 April 1865.*

Below: *Commemorative illustration of Robert E Lee's surrender to Ulysses S Grant at Appomattox Court House.*

In the Gettysburg Address he had dealt with the first question. The "honored dead," "those who gave their lives that this nation might live," were the dead of both sides: Lincoln prophesied that the nation that would arise from the war, purged by great suffering of slavery and sectionalism, would be stronger and greater than ever before. In this prophecy he was to prove right.

The second question, the meaning of the war, the meaning of great wars themselves, Lincoln spoke of in his Second Inaugural Address. There he was obliged to admit that the question defeated him, that the causes and meaning of such gigantic scourges are beyond human comprehension.

INDEX

Page numbers in italics refer to illustrations

Alexander, Edward P, General, CSA 65
Allatoona (Ga) 136, 142
Amelia Court House (Va) 155, 157
Anderson, Richard H, General, CSA 57, 65, 121
Anderson, Robert H, Major, USA 10, 12, 13, 85, 86
Antietam *42-43*, 43, 46, 91, 98, 112, 118, 155
Antietam Creek 43, *44-45*
Appomattox (battle) 80
Appomattox Court House (Va) *81*, 81, 157
Appomattox River 146
Armistead Lewis, General, CSA 125
Army of the Cumberland (USA) 67, 68, 72, 76, 134
Army of Mississippi (CSA) 92
Army of the Mississippi (USA) 92
Army of Northern Virginia (CSA) 21, 22, 28, 42, 54, 55, 65, 80, 98, 99, 112, 114, 133, 134, 152, 154, 155, 157
Army of the Ohio (USA) 92, 134
Army of the Potomac (USA) 23, 32, 42, 46, 49, 51, 54-55, *57*, 66, 98, 99, 113, 114, 115, 116, 117, 122, 125, 133, 134, 142, 152, 157
Army of Tennessee (CSA) 67, 68, 69, 76, 135, 136, 142
Army of the Tennessee (USA) 134, 140
Ashby, Turner, General, CSA 32, *40*, 40, 41
Atlanta (Ga) 71, 80, 87, 135, 138, 139, *140-141*, 141, *143*, 143, 145
Atlanta (battle) 140-141, *142*, 142

Ball's Bluff (Va) 88
Baltic (steamer) 86
Baltimore (Md) *115*, 115
Banks, Nathaniel Prentiss, General, USA 22, 23 32, 34, 35, 38, 104, 106, 111
Barksdale, William, General, CSA 49, 65, 124
Barlow, Francis, General, USA 60, 117
Baton Rouge (La) 101, 103
Beauregard, Pierre Gustave Toutant, General, CSA 10, 12, *12*, 13, 16, 17, 18, 86, 92, 94, 95, 96, *97*
Bee, Bernard, General, CSA 18
Ben Hur 92
Benton (gunboat) 102, *102-103*
Bigelow, John, Captain, USA 124
Big Black River 105, 106
Birney, David B, General, USA 121
Black Horse Cavalry *20*, 21
black troops 147-148
Blackburn's Ford 16, 17
blockade 16, *16*, 17
Boyd, Belle *35*, 35

Bragg, Braxton, General, CSA *68*, 68, 69, 71, 72, 73, 75, 76, 92, 113, 134, 135
Brandy Station (Va) 113-114
Brannan, John, General, USA 73, 75
Breckinridge, John C, General, CSA 92
Brice's Crossroads (Miss) 138
Bruinsburg (Miss) 104
Buchanan, James 10, 86
Buckner, Simon Bolivar, General, CSA 71
Buell, Don Carlos, General, USA 92, 93, 95, 96
Buford, John, General, USA 116
Bull Run (stream) 16, 18, *21*, 21
Bull Run, First Battle of 17, 60, 88, 92; Second Battle of 99, 112, 116; *see also* Manassas
Burnside, Ambrose, General, USA 46, 47, 51, 54, 64, 87, *98*, 98, 99, 133, 147, 148
Butler, Benjamin, General, USA 15

Canby, Edwin R S, General, USA *136*
Cashtown (Pa) 116, 117
Cassville (Ga) 136
casualties: at Antietam 43
at Champion's Hill 105
at Chancellorsville 65
at Chickamauga 75
at First Manassas 19
at Fort Sumter 13
at Fredericksburg 51
at Gettysburg 66, 133
at Petersburg 78, 148
at Second Manassas 29
in the Shenandoah Valley 41
at Shiloh 96
at Vicksburg 111
Cedar Creek (battle) 152, 155
Cemetery Hill *67*, 67, 117, 118, *121*, 121, 125, 127
Cemetery Ridge *119*, 119, 122, 124, 128
Centreville (Va) 16, 28, 29
Chamberlain, Joshua Lawrence, Colonel, USA 51, 122
Champion's Hill 105
Chancellorsville 57, 58, 60, 61, 64, 98, 99, 112, 114, 118, 140; battle *58*, 58-65, 66
Charleston (SC) 86
Charleston Harbor 10, 85
Chattahoochie River 138
Chattanooga (Tenn) 68, 68-69, 69, 71, 72, 73, 74, 75, 76, 78, 99, 134, 135, 136, 142
Cheatham, Benjamin, General, CSA 140
Chickahominy River 80
Chickamauga (battle) 70 (map), 71-76, *77*
Chickamauga Creek 72, 134
Chickasaws Bluffs 101
Cobb, Thomas, General, CSA 50
Cold Harbor (Va) 78, 111, 134, 146
Colville, Colonel, USA 122
Confederate States of America 10, 14, 15, 22, 27, 32, 85, 155
Corinth (Miss) 92, 94
Couch, Darius N, General, USA 64
Crittenden, Thomas L, General, USA 69, 71, 72, 96
Cross Keys (Va) 41
Crump's Landing (Tenn) 93

Culp's Hill 118, 124, 125, 129
Culpeper (Va) 23, 46, 114
Cumberland River 89
Cushing, Alonso, Lt, USA 12

Dallas (Ga) 138
Dalton (Ga) 134, 135, 136
Danville Railroad 155, 157
Davis, Jefferson 8, 9, 10, 15, 22, 42, 68, 85, 102, 104, 112, 133, 135, 138, 144, 154, 155
Davis, Jefferson C, General, USA 74
Deep Run 49
Department of Tennessee 99
Devil's Den 121, 124
"Dictator" (mortar) 149, *150-151*
Dinwiddie Court House (Va) 155
Dodge, Grenville, Captain, USA 140
Doubleday, Abner, General, USA 86, 117

8th Ohio 128
8th Pennsylvania Cavalry 60
Early, Jubal Anderson, General, CSA 57, 64, 65, 121, 124, 146, 152, 155
Elliot's Salient 147
Emancipation Proclamation 43, *46*, 46
Emmitsburg Road 128
Ewell, Richard, S, General, CSA *33*, 33, 34, 38, 41, 113, 114, 117, 118, 121, *124*, 124, 127
Ezra Church (Ga) 141, *143*, 142

1st Minnesota 124
15th Alabama 122
50th New York Engineers 152, *152*
53rd Ohio 93
Fair Oaks (Va) 80
Falling Waters (Md) 133
Farragut, David Glasgow, Admiral, USN 101, 103
Ferrero, Edward, General, USA 147, 148
Fisher's Hill (battle) 152
Five Forks (battle) 155
Forbes, Edwin 125, 147
'foot cavalry' 27, 35, *38*, 38
Forrest, Nathan Bedford, General, CSA 16, 71, 76, 87, 96, *97*, 101, 138, 141
Fort Donelson 67, 89, 111
Fort Fisher 154
Fort Henry 67, 89
Fort Johnson 86
Fort Monroe 16
Fort Moultrie *10*, 10, 12, 85
Fort Pemberton 102
Fort Stedman 152
Fort Sumter 10, *11*, *12*, 12-13, *13*, 14, 85, *86*, 86-87, *87*, 89, 92
Franklin, William B, General, USA 49
Franklin (Tenn) 142, 155
Franklin (WV) 34
Franklin's Crossing (Va) 113
Frederick (Md) 115
Fredericksburg (battle) 47 (map), *48*, *50*, 47-51, 80
Fredericksburg (Va) 46, 47, *48*, *49*, 49, *51*, 51, *52-53*, 54, 55, 57, 64, 74, 98, 112, 113, 114, 133
Fremont, John Charles, General, USA *31*, 31, 32, 33,

33, 35, 39, 41
Front Royal (Va) 35, 38, 39, 41

Gardner, Alexander 84, 119
Garnett, Richard, General, CSA 128
Gettysburg (battle) *66*, 66, *67*, 67, 69, 74, 87, 111, 116 (map), 116-133, 134, 140
Gettysburg Address 157
Gibbon, John, General, USA 116, 121, 125, 126, 128, 152
Gordon, John B, General, CSA 157
Gordonsville (Va) 22
Grand Gulf (Miss) 104, 105, 106
Granger, Gordon, General, USA 75
Grant, Ulysses S, General, USA 46, 66, 67, 75, *76*, 76, 78, 80, 281, 81, 87, *89*, 89, 92, 93, 94, *95*, 95, 96, 99, 100, 101, 102, 103, 104, 105, 106, 107, *111*, 111, 113, 134, 142, 144, 146, 147, 148, 152, 155, *157*, 157
Gregg Maxey, General, CSA 28, 49
Grierson, Benjamin H, General, USA 103
Grierson, R H, Colonel, USA 103
Groveton (Va) 28

Haines Bluff (Miss) 103
Halleck, Henry W, General, USA 92, *92*, 94, 103, 106, 111, 114, 115, 142
Hamilton's Crossing (Va) 49
Hancock, Winfield Scott, General, USA 117, 118, 121, 124, 125, 126, 128, 152
Hard Times (La) 103
Hardee, William J, General, CSA 92, 135, 139, 140, 144
Harper's Ferry (WV) 16, 35, *36-37*, 38, 39, 115
Harper's Weekly 148
Harris, I G 94
Harrisonburg (Va) 34, 38, 40
Hartranft, John, General, USA 154
Haskell, Franklin, Lt, USA 128
Hatcher's Run 154
Hazel Grove 60, 61, 64
Henry House Hill 18, 29
Heth, Henry, General, CSA 116, 117, 121, *133*
Hildebrand, General, USA 93
Hill, Ambrose Powell, General, CSA 21, 22, 23, 57, 61, 65, 113, 116, 121, 127, 146, 152, 155
Hill, Daniel Harvey, General, CSA 21, 69, 71, 72, 74, 75, 76
Holly Springs (Miss) 101
Hood, John Bell, General, CSA 57, 72, *73*, 73, 74, 76, 77, 80, 121, 122, 135, 136, 138, 139, *141*, 141, 142
Hooker, Joseph, General, USA *54*, 54, 55, 57, 58, 60, 64, 65, *87*, 98, 99, 101, *112*, 113, 114, 115
Hornet's Nest 94-95, *96*, 96
Horseshoe Ridge 72, 73, 74
Hough, Daniel, Private, USA 13, 86
Howard, Oliver Otis, General, USA 58, 60, 117, 118, 124, 125, *136*, 140, 141, 143
Humphreys, Andrew, General, USA 50
Hurlburt, Steven A, General,

USA 92, 94

Iron Brigade 116, 117, 118, 125, 152

Jackson (Miss) 104, 105, 142
Jackson (Tenn) 101
Jackson, Thomas Jonathan (Stonewall), General, CSA 14, *15*, 16, 17, 18, *19*, 19, 22, 23, 27, 28, 29, 30, *30*, 31, 32, 34, 35, 38, 39, 41, 46, 47, 49, 50, 58, *59*, *60*, 60, 61, *62-63*, *65*, 65, 87, 99, 117, 118, 152, 155
James, George S, Captain, CSA 12, 86
James Island battery 12, 86
Johnson, Edward, General, CSA 121, 125
Johnston, Albert Sidney, General, CSA 16, 87, 92, 93, *94*, 94, 96
Johnston, Joseph Eggleston, General, CSA 16, 17, 18, 19, 80, 87, 98, 102, *103*, 104, 105, 106, 113, 134, 135, 136, 138, 141, 154, 157

Keenan, Peter, Major, USA 60
Kemper, James, General, CSA 128
Kennesaw Mountain *138*, 138, 139, 142
Kernstown (Va) 32
Kilpatrick, Judson, General, USA 126
Kingston (Ga) 142

LaGrange (Tenn) 103
Lacey, B T 58
Lafayette (Ga) 71
Lake Providence 102
Ledlie, James H, General, USA 148
Lee, Fitzhugh, General, CSA 58
Lee, Robert Edward, General, CSA *14*, 14, 16, 17, 19, 20, 21, *22*, 22, 23, 27, 28, 29, 31, 32, 33, 34, 41, 42, 43, 47, 49, 51, 54, 55, 57, 58, *59*, 59, *60*, 60, 61, *64*, 64, 65, 66, 67, 75, 80, *81*, 81, 87, 98, 99, 111, 112, *113*, 113, 114, 115, 116, 117, 118, 121, 124, 125, 126, 127, 128, 133, 134, 144, 146, 152, 154, 155, *157*, 157
Lee, S D, General, CSA 141, 143
Leesburg (Va) 40
Lee's Hill 50
Lee's and Gordon's Mill 72
Lexington (gunboat) 92, *93*, 95
Lincoln, Abraham 8-10, 14, 16, 43, 46, *84*, 84, 85, 86, 87, 96, *98*, 99, 111, 112, 128, 133, 134, 141, 144, 148, 154, 155, 157
Little Round Top 121, 122, *123*, 123, 129
Logan, John A, General, USA 105
Longstreet, James, General, CSA 17, 21, 23, 27, 28, 29, 46, 47, 49, 50, 51, 57, 66, 69, 72, 73, 75, 87, 112, 113, 121, 123, 127, 129, 133
Lookout Mountain 71
Lovejoy (Ga) 141

McClellan, George B, General, USA 16, 19, 20, *21*, 21, 22, 23, 27, 28, 29, 32, 39, 42, 43, 46, 55, 87, *98*, 99, 154
McClernand, John A, General,

USA 103, *104*, 105
McCook, Edward, General, USA 96, 141
McDowell, Irwin, General, USA 16, 17, 18, 32, 34, 38, 39, 41, 87
McDowell (Va) 34
McLaws, Lafayette, General, CSA 57, 64, 121, 122
McPherson, James B, General, USA 102, 104, 105, 134, 136, *136*, 138, 139, 140, 142
McPherson's Ridge 116
Macon (Ga) 141
Malvern Hill (battle) 80
Manassas Junction (Va) 16, 17, 18 27
Manassas, First Battle of 14, 17 (map), 18, *20*, 21, 23, *24-25*, 80, 88; Second Battle of 21, 23, 27, 28 (map), *29*, 29, 30, 42, 66, 80, 98
'March to the Sea' 134-145, (map) 135
Marietta (Ga) 138
Marye's Hill/Heights 49, *50*, 50, 64, 65
Maryland Guard, *43*, 43
Massanutten Mountains 34, 35
Meade, George M, General, USA 78, 87, 115, 116, 117, 118, 119, 121, 122, 124, 125, 126, 127, 129, 130-131, 134, 148, 157
Melcher, H S, Lt, USA 122
Memphis (Tenn) 99, 101
Meredith, Solomon J, General, USA 116
Mexican War 68, 75
Middletown (Va) 35
Milroy, R H, General, USA 34, 38, 114
Milliken's Bend 102, 103
Mississippi River 67, 88, 96, 99, 101, 102, 111
'Mud March' 51
Mudge, Charles R, Colonel, USA 125
Murfreesboro (Tenn) 67, 69

Nashville (Tenn) 92, 142
Nast, Thomas 144
Nelson, William 'Bull', General, USA 94, 95, 96
New Orleans (La) 101
New York Zouaves 18
Newton, John, General, USA 121
North Anna 79, 134

114th Pennsylvania *149*, 149
140th New York 122
Orchard Knob (battle of) *74-75*, 75
Owl Creek 92

Patterson, Robert, General, USA 16
Peach Orchard 121, *122*, 122
Peachtree Creek 138
Pelham, John, Major, USA 49
Pemberton, John Clifford, General, CSA *101*, 101, 102, 103, 104, 105, 106
Pender, William Dorsey, General, CSA 49, 116, 121
Peninsular Campaign 19, 43, 80
Pennsylvania Bucktails 38, *38-39*
Petersburg (Va) 78, 80, 87, 134, 146, *146-147*, 147, *148*,

148, *149*, 149, *152*, 152, *153*, 153, 154, 155, *156*, 156
Pettigrew, J Johnston, General, CSA 127, 128, 133
Philadelphia Zouaves 84, *85*
Pickett, George Edward, General, CSA *126*, 126, 127-128, 133, 155
Pickett's Charge *127*, 127, 128, 129, 133
Pipe Creek 116
Pittsburg Landing (Tenn) 92, 93, 94, 95
Plank Road 58
Pleasants, Henry, Colonel, USA 147
Pleasonton, Alfred, General, USA 60, 114
Polk, Leonidas, General, CSA 71, 72, 73, 92, 135, 136, 138
Pope, John, General, USA 19, 20, 22, *23*, 23, 27, 28, 29, 87
Port Gibson (Miss) 104, 106, 111
Port Hudson (Miss) 104, 106, 111
Port Republic (Va) 41
Porter, David Dixon, Admiral, USN *102*, 102, 103, 154
Potomac River 35, 38
Prentiss, Benjamin M, General, USA 92, 93, 94
Pryor, Roger A, (CSA) 12

Rapidan River 57, 64
Rappahannock River 26, *26-27*, 27, 47, 51, *52-53*, 55, 57, 64, 65
Raymond (Miss) 105
Red River 102
Red River Campaign 104
Reed's Bridge 72
Reed, C W 122
Resaca (Ga) 136, *137*, 142
Reynolds, John R, General, USA 73, 115, 116, *117*, 117, 121
Richmond (Va) 18, 19, 22, 23, 28, 29, 32, *78*, 78, 80, 114, 115, 136, 146, 149, 155, *156*, 157
Ringgold (Ga) 136
Rodes, Robert, General, CSA 121
Romney (Va) 32
Rosecrans, William Starkie, General, USA 68, 69, *70*, 70, 71, 72, 73, 74, 76, 101, 113, 134, 136
Round Top 121, 122, 124, 126 *see also* Little Round Top
Ruggles, Daniel, General, CSA 94

2nd Massachusetts 125
7th New York Cavalry *55*, 55
16th Wisconsin 93
Salem Church 65
Savannah (Ga) 80, 144
Savannah (Tenn) 92, 93, 94, 95
Saylor's Creek 157
Schenck, Robert C, General, USA 34, 38
Schofield, John, General, USA 134, 136, 138, 141, 142, 155
Schurz, Carl, General, USA 117
Scott, Winfield, General, USA 86
secession 8, 10, 14, 85, 86-87
Sedgwick, John, General, USA 57, 64, 65, 121
Seminary Ridge 116, 117, 126
Seven Days (battle) 19, 20, 29,

41
Seward, William 86
Sharpsburg (Md) 43
Shenandoah River 35
Shenandoah Valley 16, *17*, 17, 30, 31, 32, 34, 38, 41, 46, 152, 155
Shenandoah Valley Campaign (of Jackson) 19, 27, 29, 30, 31, 32 (map), 33-41
Sheridan, Philip, General, USA 74, 80, *81*, 81, 87, 152, *154*, *155*, 155, 157
Sherman, William Tecumseh, General, USA 13, 76, 80, 87, *88*, 88, 92, 93, 101, 102, 103, 104, 105, 106, 111, 134, 135, *136*, 136, 138, *139*, 139, 141, 142, *144*, 144, 155, 157
Shields, James, General, USA 32, 41
Shiloh 67, (map) *88*, 92-97
Shirley House *104*, 104
Sickles, Daniel E, General, USA 58, 60, 117, 121, 122, 125
Signal Hill 18
slavery 8, 10, 84
Slocum, Henry W, General, USA 117, 118, 125, *136*
Snake Creek Gap 136
South Side Railroad 152, 155
Spotsylvania (Va) 78, 134, 146
states' rights doctrine 84
Steel's Bayou 102
Stoneman, George, General, USA 141
Stone's River (Tenn) 67
Stonewall Brigade 18, 32, 39, 41, *60*, 60, *61*, 61
Stony Ridge (Manassas) 28
Strasburg (Va) 32, 34, 35, 41
Stuart, David, Colonel, USA 93, 94
Stuart, James Ewell Brown, General, USA 18, 21-22, 23, 27, 43, 46, 54, *56*, 57, 58, 61, 64, 87, 113, 114-115, 118, 128, 155
Sturgis, Samuel D, General, USA 138
Sumner, Edwin 47, 49, 50
Swift Run Gap (Va) 34
Sykes, George, General, USA 122, 125

20th Maine 122
21st Missouri 93
24th Michigan 118
25th Missouri 93
36th Pennsylvania *55*, 55
Tallahatchie River 102
Taylor, Richard, General, CSA 41
Terry, Alfred H, General, USA *136*
Tennessee River 67, 71, 89, 92, 94, 95, 96
Thomas, George H, General, USA 69, 72, 73, 74, 75, 76, 80, 87, 134, *136*, 138, 141, 142
Trimble, Isaac R, General, CSA 127
Trostle's Farm *124*, 124
Tullahoma (Tenn) 69
Tyler (gunboat) 92, *93*, 95

United States Ford 58

Van Dorn, Earl, General, CSA 96, 101
Van Pelt, Lt, USA *72*, 73
Vicksburg 67, 69, 87, 113, 134, 146; siege and battle 99, 100

(map), 101-111
Vincent, Strong, Colonel, USA
122
Virginia Military Institute 31

Wadsworth, James, General,
USA 117
Walker, W H T, General, CSA
71
Wallace, Lew, General, USA
92, 93, 96

Wallace, W H M, General, USA
92, 94
Warren, Gouveneur, General,
USA 122, 152, 155
Warrenton Turnpike 16, 18, 19
Warrenton (Va) 46
Washington, DC 18, 20, *28*, 29,
32, 85, 114, 115, 152
Waud, Alfred R 21, 28, 139, 148
Weldon Railroad 146, 152
Welles, Gideon 133

West Point 12, 14, 16, 17, 31
Western and Atlantic Railroad
136
Wheat Field 121
Wheeler, Joseph, General, USA
135, 136, 139, 140, 141
White Oak Swamp 115
Whitman, Walt 80
Wigfall L, Louis 13
Wilderness 57, 58, 78, 80, 134,
146

Wilderness Tavern 58
Winchester (Va) 32, 35, 38, 152
Wood, T J, General, USA 73,
74, 75
Wrightsville (Pa) *114*, 114
Wyeth, N C 78

Yazoo Pass 102
Yazoo River 101, 102
Young's Point 102